D1171058

THURSDAY ISLAND NURSE

Also by Elizabeth Burchill

New Guinea Nurse
Innamincka
Labrador Memories

THURSDAY ISLAND NURSE

ELIZABETH BURCHILL,

S.R.N, R.M., T.C.

RIGBY

RIGBY LIMITED • ADELAIDE • SYDNEY
MELBOURNE • BRISBANE • PERTH

First published 1972
Copyright © 1972 Elizabeth Burchill
Library of Congress Catalog Card Number 71-141709
National Library of Australia Registry Card
Number and ISBN 0 85179 302 9

Wholly designed and set up in Australia
Printed by Dai Nippon Printing Co. (International) Ltd, Hong Kong

CONTENTS

LIST OF ILLUSTRATIONS

All photographs are by Jocelyn Burt except where indicated

FOREWORD

By H. J. Winterbottom, M.B. B.S. (Melbourne)

I am honoured to be asked to write a Foreword for *Thursday Island Nurse*. Sister D. E. Burchill has been a member of the nursing profession for many years and some of the most rewarding periods of this time have been spent with the native peoples of Australia, New Guinea, and the Torres Strait Islands. She has devoted much effort in helping them not only with their illnesses, but also to live healthier lives.

I knew Sister Burchill at Thursday Island where she was Maternal and Child Welfare Clinic Sister, and she spared no effort in helping the mothers look after their babies, instructing them in their care and feeding.

She used to follow up all her cases, even to going to the homes of those who were failing to attend the Clinic, thus ensuring that all under her guidance received the proper care.

As a result of her interest in these people, she learned many of their problems, and got to understand them in a way few people could, and particularly so as a result of visiting them in their homes.

Her writings on the Torres Strait Islands and their people should be full of human and ethnological interest, and I am sure that the readers will derive much pleasure and benefit from them.

Kingaroy, Queensland.

1

THE SUPREME EVENT

THE TWENTY ISLANDS of the Thursday Island group are scattered across the 130 miles of sea between Cape York, on the extreme northern tip of Australia, and the coast of Papua. It is an area that is associated with most of the great explorers who charted the seacoast of Australia, and has a colourful historical background. The area now has tremendous potential for tourism.

Less than a century ago, the people of the islands were living in Stone Age conditions, and those few people who knew anything about them spoke of their savagery, tribal warfare, headhunting and cannibalism. They came under Australian administration in 1872, the year in which the Islands were added to the Colony of Queensland.

The Torres Strait Islanders are a distinct race, more akin to the Papuans farther north than to the Australian Aborigines, from whom they are very different in physique and personality. They are strong and capable, taller and finer in features than the dark-skinned people of some other parts of Australia. Newcomers remark admiringly on the magnificent appearance of the tall, warrior-type of men, with their handsome and carefree women and winsome, chocolate-coloured babies.

In the past, these men had a fearsome reputation as fighting men, and even dared to attack a British man o' war in broad daylight; a feat which earned the name of Warrior Island for their home island. Terrible stories of the murder of traders and shipwrecked sailors filtered through to civilisation, and to the ardent missionaries of that era it seemed that the area must be a "field ripe for the harvesting."

The first missionaries to brave the islands were members of the London Missionary Society, an undenominational organisation which accepted the challenge of spreading Christianity southwards from the foothold which it had gained in Papua. The L.M.S., as it is generally called, decided to send out Pacific Islanders who had been baptised at Melanesian missions in childhood. These men had a real missionary zeal, and being coloured themselves were often more acceptable to tribesmen of the Pacific area than were white missionaries. They gained experience by teaching at mission stations attached to the Queensland sugar plantations, which in those days employed many Kanakas from the islands.

Samoan missionaries and trained teachers landed first on Daun Island, in the east of the group, and on Darnley Island in the west, on 1 July 1871. This day is commemorated every year by the Islanders.

The missionaries had a hard time to begin with. The islands were truly pagan, and in most cases a stranger was killed instantly. Men slept with their weapons in hand, prepared to fight for their lives. It was a crime for anyone to awaken the chief of the tribe, and if a crying child woke him it was killed and eaten. The first missionary who called such a chief to prayer paid for his boldness with his life.

But the supreme faith of the missionaries slowly overcame the suspicions of the Islanders, and once they had been accepted they were able to make rapid progress. The Islanders were quick to absorb the new teaching and having embraced Christianity they gave up headhunting and heathen worship.

2

Early Christian pioneers in the Straits,* the Reverend James Chalmers (whom the Islanders called Tamate) and the Reverend S. McFarlane, were killed by natives in New Guinea but nowadays their names are frequently given to small children. The L.M.S. worked in the area from 1871 until 1915. The first step to leave the Torres Straits was taken in 1914 when the organisation asked the Church of England, already established on Thursday Island, to take over the administration. With the pressures of war it was a grave financial undertaking for the Church of England as well, but they accepted the opportunity and the L.M.S. relinquished its buildings. The Islanders were confronted with a new way of worshipping; they saw for the first time altar candles, vestments, incense, and were involved in confession rites and Church of England ritual. The handing over of the people of the Torres Straits, without choice, has not gone without comment by writers concerned with the history of north Australia.

Not all writing was critical, however, and *Round About The Torres Straits* by Bishop White, ecclesiastical head of the diocese, puts forward the Church of England story.

He wrote: "When I first came to Thursday Island in 1900 I confess to casting very covetous eyes on the surrounding islands. They were so near, so convenient to visit from the centre of the diocese, inhabited by a people so attractive and full of interest that I wished with all my heart we had them under our care."

Fifteen years later Bishop White saw his dream fulfilled.

He set out on a tour of the islands in 1915 to prepare the people for change and took with him the Reverend E. J. Nash, the Reverend F. Walker, and selected Islanders. The Reverend Nash was an Englishman who, on his return to England, named his house "Waiben," the native name for Thursday Island. The Reverend Walker was a L.M.S.

* The official name of "Torres Strait" is used throughout the book where it refers to the body of water between Cape York and the Papuan coast. "Torres Straits," when used by itself, refers to the islands in the Strait as a geographical area.

3

missionary. Appropriately their ship was the L.M.S. vessel *Goodwill*.

They stopped first at Yam Island. This was the home of Maino, son of Kebiscu, who had been a great native chief in the early days of missionary work in the Straits. The L.M.S. missionaries converted Maino to Christianity and he helped capture the last of the headhunters.

When the Governor of New Guinea, Sir William McGregor, visited the Islands, Maino was his loyal body-guard. In appreciation the governor in his will left Maino an annuity of a hundred dollars for life. Maino died in 1939. He was buried with ceremony and the epitaph on the white headstone reads: MAINO. THE LAST OF THE WARRIORS. HE FEARED GOD ABOVE ALL OTHERS.

On Darnley Island the L.M.S. had built a church of limestone from the reefs. The church service was partly in English and partly in native language and the Church of England planned to give instruction and later hold confirmation services. Church wardens and lay readers were to replace the deacons and the duties of each were explained to the Islanders.

On Murray Island one hundred and fifty of the four hundred and fifty residents were churchgoers. Badu Island was the last island to be visited. Before the missionary era in the Straits it was the home of warring tribes but when Bishop White landed for the first time, he was approached only by an anxious old man. For forty years he had acted as official "church wakener" for the L.M.S.; with an ancient silver-topped black rod he prodded churchgoers who fell asleep during the sermons by native deacons. The old man liked his job and wanted to keep it.

At a Testimony Meeting on one of the islands an old man described the work of the L.M.S.: "The Gospel of Jesus Christ has come like dynamite, shattered old evil customs, killed them dead, just like when dynamite is exploded in the water to kill all the fish around."

In 1917 the Church of England opened a theological training college on Moa Island. Four Islanders graduated, were ordained, and thereafter addressed as "Father." They preached, taught, and performed the sacraments under the supervision of a presiding priest who visited the island to which they were sent.

Joseph Lui, one of the Islanders accompanying the bishop on his first tour of the diocese, spoke five languages. He had become a top pearl diver but chose to train for the new clergy.

The first priest graduated from the college in 1925 and priests subsequently graduating from the Moa Island Theological College have been sent to missions farther afield. In due course the Roman Catholic Church was established, with a church building and school. A Presbyterian Church was built too and residents of the Torres Straits have fond memories of Sunday School teacher, Jean Ling. She was an eighteen-year-old Malayan who left the Torres Straits to travel throughout Queensland as Peanut Princess. After promoting peanut products she trained at St Andrew's Hospital in Brisbane for three years to become a nurse. Married to an English businessman she now lives in Melbourne.

2

EPIC YEARS

IN ABOUT THE MIDDLE of the nineteenth century, adventurous white men discovered that the tropical waters of the Strait fed the largest oyster shell beds in the world. The lustrous mother-of-pearl lining of these shells was acclaimed as Australia's most valuable maritime product. A vigorous pearl shell industry developed. Tons of first class shell were exported to the mainland and overseas for the making of buttons, studs, and novelties.

The first headquarters of this Torres Strait industry was at Somerset on the Cape York Peninsula but the anchorage was so poor that the site did not develop as expected. Towards the end of 1877 the Government settlement was moved from Somerset to Thursday Island.

The new site possessed a splendid harbour and was becoming of increasing strategic importance but the pearl shell industry was about the only reason for a European establishment in such a remote area. To advise traders and others of the change an announcement appeared in Queensland newspapers in 1878 saying that the Government settlement was officially opened and that the Torres Strait mailboats would call at Thursday Island instead of Somerset.

The settlement was primarily for government staff and Thursday Island became the most northerly administration centre on the continent to fly the Australian flag. Divers, traders and others engaged in the pearling industry were encouraged to settle on adjacent islands. Thursday Island became the "big city" and a town reservoir, stone jetty, two banks, shops, government buildings, and private houses soon appeared. The Island itself is tiny, being only about a square mile in area, and it is surrounded by Prince of Wales Island (the largest in the group), Hammond, Horn, Friday, and Goode Island.

No one seems to know how Thursday Island received its name but it was not used in any publication before an Admiralty chart of 1850. Over the years the name has been abbreviated commonly to T.I.

Romantically described by various writers as the "Gibraltar of Australia," "Pearl of the Pacific," "Queen of the Sea," "Paradise of the North," and "Jewel of the Coral Sea," Thursday Island is the gateway to the Torres Strait. It has the best anchorage between Australia and New Guinea.

The first white child was born on the Island soon after the settlement began. She grew up to become a nun, held high office in her religious order and in 1959, as Mother Albert, celebrated the golden jubilee of her profession in Queensland.

One of the most illustrious residents of Thursday Island was the Honourable John Douglas, former premier of Queensland, and first government resident on the island. He was a man to be feared by unscrupulous traders or anyone who engaged in dishonest tactics. A chapel in the Anglican cathedral and the main street were named after him.

Much of the land of Thursday Island is concentrated on two hills. Soon after the settlement was formed, the government of Queensland established a defence outpost against enemy action because practically all shipping from the East to Australia passed through the Strait. A very substantial fort was built on the highest of the two hills.

The first garrison of Queensland soldiers stationed there was replaced by many others over the next forty years but the fort was abandoned in 1939. The great guns pointing so menacingly out to sea had never fired a single shot in anger. Older residents recall that the only sound of guns heard from the hilltop fort was the regular one o'clock time signal which exploded over the little town each day.

The barrack buildings were demolished and shipped off to become part of the military port, Darwin, the "front door" of Australia in the Northern Territory.

The massive underground section, the huge concrete gun emplacements, the three rusted seven-inch guns remaining will remind future generations of Thursday Island's strategic importance at the top of Australia. Two generations of young soldiers, awaiting combat that never came, have scratched their initials and QX Army numbers on the concrete. The manufacturer's date of 1808 can be observed on the abandoned guns, and a battered steel helmet remains, a popular relic used by photographers to provide suitable atmosphere for sightseers who visit the old fort.

During the dark days of the second World War the Australian troops once again occupied the Island and were accommodated in private houses and other available buildings. When Japanese forces threatened the safety of the Queensland coast, residents were given twenty-four hours' notice to evacuate and permission to carry only two suitcases.

Army occupation lasted four years and public and private property deteriorated in upkeep or were destroyed. The Metropole Hotel in the main street was burnt to the ground so that only the front steps remained. The town's only printing press was lost, never recovered and never replaced. Instead of the printed page, carbon copies of the local weekly paper *Torres Strait News* were made and circulated.

The dirt roads on Thursday Island are notoriously bad and one wonders why the manpower and heavy equipment available during the war were not used to build good sealed roads; a legacy that might have served as compensation for damage done.

Residents on returning to the Island found former homes needlessly damaged and ransacked. In spite of government aid it was an experience from which they may take many years to recover.

Much of the meagre land of Thursday Island is still reserved for defence purposes but there is little likelihood that it will be used for military or naval purposes again. It is the main reason for the housing difficulties with which the Island is plagued.

The town area of the Island is as picturesque as any tourist resort. Douglas Street is a wide tree-lined thoroughfare with some fine modern shops strangely contrasted against shabby and dilapidated buildings.

Victoria Parade, running parallel to the waterfront, is the scene of constant pearling activity. When a lugger arrives in port tons of valuable pearl shells are carried ashore in big, long-handled wooden boxes to be graded, weighed, and packed for export at warehouses on the parade.

The Federal Hotel, a two-storeyed building on the parade, is a well-known landmark of one of the earliest pioneers, Thomas McNulty, who resigned from the Queensland Police Force to try his luck on Thursday Island. He bought an hotel building at an auction sale in Queensland, had it demolished and shipped to Thursday Island. In 1897 when there were less than a hundred residents on the Island he opened the first hotel in town, the Thursday Island Hotel, which later became Tattersall's Hotel. When the building was burnt down in 1899 Thomas McNulty built his hotel on the waterfront and gave it the present name of the Federal Hotel. McNulty's hotels have always been popular tarrying places for writers, adventurers, and businessmen.

Thomas McNulty's only surviving child, Maggie, who

was raised on the Island, lived there in retirement for many years. When I first met her, in 1960, she was in her eighties and given to reminiscing about the early days of the settlement and the guests of her father's hotel.

The Fifty Year Jubilee celebrations of 1927 are still remembered by the old residents. They talk of the floats, the national costumes of the Thursday Island residents who had lived previously in other parts of the world, and the pioneers from Somerset on Cape York.

One visitor, Captain Frank Hurley, shinned up the roof of a building to take photographs. He commented later that. it was the best street procession he had seen for the size of the town.

An interesting relic put on display for visitors was the four-wheel phaeton from the garrison in which Lord Kitchener had once been driven around the town.

A grey, stone obelisk is lit up at night in Douglas Street. It honours Joseph Teatham Wassell who was doctor on the Island for fifteen years. He was responsible for reducing the incidence of Beri Beri, a vitamin deficiency disease now almost unknown, to a four per cent low of known cases. He had in his care more than 5,000 Japanese, Malays, Chinese, and a great assortment of mixed bloods engaged in the pearling industry. Torres Strait Islanders were not allowed to live on T.I. until after the second World War. With about six ships arriving in port each week quarantine regulations were strictly enforced. Dr Wassell died when he was only forty after he cut his foot on the poisoned coral of a jagged reef.

Nowadays about 2,500 people, mostly Torres Strait Islanders, Malayans and those of mixed blood live in the township, on T.I. White people employed by the government or engaged in private enterprise number three to four hundred. Few tourists visit the remote area of the Torres Strait. Most of the commercial goods are from the mainland and are priced according to freight charges which can be considerable. It is possible for two dollars a week to be added to the food bill of a family of four if meat is airfreighted.

Though remote from the mainland of Australia, T.I. has more than 200 telephones and an automatic radio system for world-wide communication. On the south-western end of the Island, the department of Overseas Telegraph Communication keeps in touch with near-by ships and aircraft twenty-four hours a day.

3

TORRES STRAIT MEDICAL SERVICES

THE FIRST INSTITUTION in the Torres Straits for the care of the sick was St Andrew's Cottage Hospital. It was established on T.I. by the Roman Catholic Church, but it was closed after a few years.

The Thursday Island General Hospital, with accommodation for 200 in-patients, is situated in the south-western end of the town on a spectacular promontory known as Hospital Point. It has bungalow-type buildings that act as familiar landmarks for sea travellers. Passengers and crew lining the decks are within waving distance of hospital staff members and convalescent patients, and always exchange greetings.

For an outpost establishment the hospital is well staffed and equipped. It serves the sixteen inhabited islands of the strait with an efficient radio network and, through its mother station at T.I., top priority is given to the medical calls which are relayed to the hospital. When such a call is received, doctor and nurse may have to travel in a government launch to one of the islands, and bring the patient back to the hospital. It is very similar to the mainland's

Flying Doctor Service, except that boats, instead of aircraft, are used.

White and coloured patients occupy the same wards and receive equal medical attention.

In a sea community like that of T.I. one of the most common diseases is Diver's Paralysis. The condition, commonly called the "bends," is the result of nitrogen bubbles in the blood stream when the diver works at great ocean depths.

Several years ago a modern midwifery building was opened by the wife of the governor of Queensland, Lady Lavarack. The building was named after her and a silver cup donated for the first baby born in the new block. The hospital at one time was a training school for nurses and local girls were able to train there. After three years, candidates sat for state examinations in Brisbane. Nowadays, qualified nurses are recruited from the mainland.

Selected Torres Strait Island girls made excellent nursing aides, quietly, cheerfully, efficiently performing their duties as they moved barefooted through the T.I. hospital wards. They dressed in a fawn cotton uniform with white collar, cuffs, and traditional nurse's cap, and lived near the hospital in modern nurses' quarters erected in 1954.

In off-duty hours the girls enjoyed singing, playing guitars, and performing traditional dances in Island dress. European-trained nurses lived in a group of houses close to the hospital. One of these was the former residence of the Honourable John Douglas. It was surrounded by towering coconut trees which bent lightly in the trade winds, sweet-smelling frangipani, and wild almond trees. Through the broad windows of the enclosed verandahs there were magnificent, commanding views of the harbour. Before the turn of the century Governors-General, explorers, missionaries, prominent military men, authors, and naturalists had gathered on the verandahs and in the spacious grounds. The historical house eventually fell into disrepair and was rebuilt to serve the needs of present day nurses.

Some doctors and nurses have put in long terms of service at T.I. Hospital. The original matron, friend of the Honourable John Douglas, trained at the famous Edinburgh Infirmary, Scotland, in Lord Lister's day, and continued to live on the Island after retirement. Another matron who stayed on the Island for seventeen years was awarded the Royal Red Cross for her work with an operating theatre unit during the first World War.

A cousin of mine, whose father was at one time town clerk of Normanton in the Gulf Country of Queensland, was matron at the T.I. Hospital during the devastating Spanish influenza epidemic of 1919. Her sister trained as a nurse at the hospital.

One of the doctors, Dr G. M. Vernon, stayed eleven years and was affectionately known as "Doc." He loved music, was organist at the Anglican cathedral, and had a keen interest in animal welfare, football, cricket, and aquatic sports. He was an active member of the Returned Soldiers' League and had been awarded the Military Cross for courageous conduct in Egypt in the first World War. He was also founder, secretary, and life member of the Thursday Island branch of the Royal Geographical Society. This was disbanded in later years.

The spirit of the man is revealed in his unpublished memoirs:

> One does not usually associate laughter with the precincts of the general hospital where there is affliction and weakness but Torres Strait Islanders, with their happy carefree natures, were freely given to this natural medicine. When death comes to the sick, the aged, and the little child, it seems to come in a gentler form to those whose skins are darker, whose lives are simpler. Perhaps nature protects those who are closer to her. Perhaps their perceptions are less keen, their hold on life less eager.

Another extract reads:

> A new boy from the Mapoon Mission on the mainland was employed by a T.I. businessman and had been employed to help in the yard. All went well until one weekend. Early on Sunday morning Charlie, as the new

boy was called, refused to use the axe, saying, "I no chop wood on Sunday. I belonga God." Then he walked off to the boy house and rolled himself in his blanket. "I'll fix him!" the boss said to his wife. The early morning hours rolled by without Charlie being approached. Presently Darkie strolled across to the kitchen and looked in the window where the boss's wife was working. She did not look responsive, so Darkie hung around hopefully trying to catch her eye. When that failed, he thought it time to exert himself. "I wanta alonga breakfast, missus," he said, reproachfully. Suddenly aware of his presence, she replied, "Oh, do you? Well, I no cook breakfast on Sunday. I belong to God." He stared, presently went away and had a big think. After a long silence, the sound of wood chopping broke the Sabbath stillness and later Charlie sat down to breakfast, a much wiser boy.

Thursday Island is the home of many European ex-nurses with children of their own. As the wives of doctors, government officials, engineers, and professional fishermen they are on hand for hospital emergencies.

Away from T.I., Torres Strait Islanders, like the native women of New Guinea, pull on rope hanging from ceiling rafters during labour in their homes. The day after the baby's birth, the mother lies in the ocean to aid expulsion of blood clots remaining in the birth canal.

Of the first triplets born in the history of the Torres Straits, two infants were identical twins delivered by a native woman. None survived. They died of a rare blood disease within three days of birth.

Like all native people, the Islanders have specific ways that have been handed down by forebears, for treating the sick. Modern medicine is easily available but natural medicines are still favoured by some of the Islanders. Natural oil from the dugong is used for medicinal purposes. It is used in the treatment of tuberculosis.

Coconut oil is used on adults and babies. If a young baby suffered from "wind" the mother rubbed the navel with oil and to reduce baby fever, rubbed the whole body with it.

15

When breast milk and clinic food were not available, milk from the green coconut was used. From the coconut palm, most benign of all island trees, nature provided a feeding bottle containing a quantity of sterile liquid suitable for early infant consumption. These young green nuts supplied adequate nourishment to sustain an island baby during the first two months of life. The baby sucked from a funnel-like teat, shaped from a particular tree leaf. It went into the small hole at the top of the coconut. The baby drank sufficient to satisfy immediate needs. Later, cooked brains and tender liver of the dugong would be added to the liquid diet. Still later, the soft, fluffy kernel of ripe coconut cooked like a potato, would be introduced to the growing child.

A smooth, rounded dugong bone provided a satisfying teething ring, and yellow and cream "money" cowries were strung together to make the child's first rattle.

In 1959 a young deep sea diver suffered severe abdominal pains while the pearling lugger was anchored out at sea. When he reached T.I. Hospital, peritonitis had developed. His life was saved by immediate surgery but the experience of the diver made such a strong impression on fellow workers that some demanded to have their unoffending appendix removed before taking to sea again.

The waters around Hospital Point are noted for the presence of sharks that congregate where there are ships and refuse finds its way into the sea. One woman fishing off the rocks at Hospital Point with a shark line and special hook caught a shark six feet long. The belly was cut open to reveal six baby sharks, each nearly a foot in length and ready to be born. Their scrambling movements were ended.

One link with the past readily seized upon by tourists and nurses new to the island is the old visitors' book at the hospital. A large, shabby volume, it dates from 1894 to 1942, the year it was put away for safe keeping. One of the early signatures belongs to Bishop White, the first Bishop of Carpentaria. He added alongside his signature: "Observed everything in perfect order."

In 1899, the government Administrator of New Guinea wrote: "I have seen the Papuan ward which seems all that could be desired except that I think a wooden floor would be more suitable."

A few years later John Henry, C.M.G., wrote: "The establishment and management of this excellent institution speaks well for the humanity and intelligence of those directing affairs at Thursday Island."

Another visitor observed simply: "Of all the way out places in North Queensland, Thursday Island is the least known."

The Chief of Staff in the Boer War, Lord Kitchener, left his signature in the visitors' book after he had been ashore to investigate defence measures before the outbreak of the first World War.

Another timely visit was that of Sir Mayo Robson, a London medical specialist, who did valuable pioneer work on the stomach and liver. His brief visit coincided with the admission to the T.I. Hospital of a patient suffering from an unusual abdominal complaint.

Two visitors who addressed the Royal Geographical Society were the doctor and politician, Sir Raphael Cilento, who is father of the present day actress Diane Cilento, and the arctic explorer, Sir Hubert Wilkins. Their signatures remain along with those of Jean B. Flynn, who is the widow of "Flynn of the Inland", Alan Vickers, who was president of the Royal Flying Doctor Service, and Edith Kerr, a Presbyterian missionary from Korea on leave.

In 1916 the H.M.S. *Sydney* anchored in the harbour and crew members went ashore. One sailor left this in the visitors' book: "The deaf and dumb only retain their hearts. Beware all ye who are not so afflicted."

Another entry of that year reads: "July 15th, 1916. Somerset Maugham, London. Residents of T.I. tell how the author visited the wards, met a long term patient, a fiery Irishman, and asked if there were plenty of books. It is said that the Irishman looked him in the eyes, banged a clenched fist on the bedside table and thundered, 'Books! Books! I don't want books, sir. I live!'"

The most dramatic entries are the last ones; those written in 1942 following the compulsory evacuation of civilians.

17

Sister Francis was the only member of the nursing staff to remain behind at the hospital. She was officially appointed to hand over the establishment to the incoming army medical authorities.

Sister Francis wrote on 10 July 1942: "After thirteen years on this beautiful tropical island I find myself the only European woman in residence on this day."

Beneath her entry, the last one from an American army doctor is added in gratitude: "The hospitality and relaxation enjoyed in and around the Thursday Island Hospital is the first touch of genuine pleasure I have experienced in my long journey. Captain Kidshaw and Sister Francis are to be congratulated for maintaining this hospital service under such difficult times of war and isolation.

Dr Veigel Steel, San Antonio, Texas.
Captain, M.C.   U.S.A. Army."

4

ADVENTUROUS NURSING

ALTHOUGH NOT LONG BACK from a rewarding four years service as Sister-in-Charge of the government Infant Welfare Clinic in Darwin, I was beginning to feel restless.

A Melbourne newspaper advertisement stirred me to action. I cut short a proposed tour to New Zealand and applied for the Sister-in-Charge position that had been advertised by the Thursday Island Hospital Board. I was accepted and signed on for two years to work in the Maternal and Child Welfare Department.

My knowledge of Thursday Island was very limited. I was aware that it was situated at the top of Australia, somewhere between the Gulf of Carpentaria and New Guinea, and that it was a centre for pearl diving. Friends were even less informed. One declared that I could get there only by flying boat, another that the population was made up of coloured deep sea divers and fishermen. I knew that I was being employed to care for mothers and babies so the latter piece of information was discarded.

The clerk at the city airways office informed me that his company terminated northern flights at Cairns in north

Queensland. He announced blandly that another company took over from there and phoned the other office for me. "That booking office says there is no need to book a seat to Thursday Island. In the past five years that man hasn't booked a passenger!" he said.

For a time I was apprehensive but the mood soon changed and when it was time for me to leave Melbourne in 1959 for the little known Thursday Island, I was cheerful.

It was a long uneventful hop from Melbourne to Cairns where I stayed overnight before boarding another aircraft for Horn Island in the Torres Strait. Horn Island is the most northerly airfield in Australia. The plane was met by an airline chartered bus that took passengers the two miles to a stone jetty. From there a launch travelled three miles to Thursday Island.

I fell into conversation with a middle-aged couple from Sydney visiting their daughter and son-in-law who was employed as an officer with Overseas Telegraph Communications. They went to Thursday Island each year—it was an enchanted island for them.

But as I stood on the launch carrying passengers, cargo, and bags of mail, and looked out at a small rugged island with bare hills and rocks right down to the water line, doubts began to crowd my mind. Two years *here*! I suddenly felt something like dismay.

At the Thursday Island Wharf I was welcomed by hospital officials and taken by car to the other end of the island and the cottage that was to be my home for the next two years. I shared it with the hospital housekeeper, a pharmacist, and a relieving radiographer—a charming New Zealand girl, Marie, on a working holiday of Australia.

She had answered a newspaper advertisement for the temporary position and we became good friends. She was devoted to cats and acquired a jet black kitten which she called "Velvet." That cat proved to be interested in everything but leaving the house. When we shamelessly teased the animal to the point of over-excitement, Velvet would bare her teeth, snarl like a tiger cub, and leap forward into the air like a flying fish pursued by a larger fish.

20

One of its favourite tricks was clambering up a three feet high cane laundry basket and suddenly surprising us by peeping over the top.

Unfortunately Velvet was a she and tender-hearted Marie vehemently declared she could not bear the thought of her pet's litters being wantonly destroyed. Cats were plentiful on T.I. so one day Marie decided to have the cat made barren before she grew too big.

A young doctor, who was no lover of cats, agreed to perform the simple operation and, like a human patient, Velvet had nothing to eat for some hours before the event. She was in the pink of condition, having enjoyed a daily diet of raw meat and milk to which vitamins were added. In this state she went trustingly to her doom. She died under the anaesthetic before surgery began. It was whispered that there was more to that death than was immediately obvious. The doctor was known to have protested about the number of cats in the town.

A middle-aged Malayan drove me each morning to the town clinic which was about a mile and a half away. The Maternal and Infant Welfare Clinic had once been a shop but the building in Douglas Street had been bought by the government and been converted into a large waiting room, an office equipped with weighing scales, table, chairs, wash hand basin and a smaller adjoining room for the feeding of infants. Although I was answerable to the hospital board, which included the medical superintendent, the matron of the hospital, and the secretary, I revelled in the freedom of a "one woman show."

The way of life might appear unexciting and unprofitable to academic members of the profession enjoying advantages of city nursing, but to a nurse who felt the lure of far away places, the simple life of an island clinic was a satisfying experience; an adventure in nursing that became woven into the tapestry of the mind.

I worked regular hours at the town clinic, walked to every home where there were young children, visited the hospital weekly to talk with mothers of new born babies, and made fortnightly trips by sea to Horn and Hammond Islands.

In the Torres Straits there is no winter and Thursday Island enjoys one of the best climates in the world for nine months of the year; temperatures hover in the seventies and eighties, trade winds gently blow to offset humidity, and there is an annual rainfall of sixty inches. Monsoonal rains with gales and torrential rains alternate with periods of heat and calm for three months of the year.

Padding quietly on the dusty pavements of Thursday Island are people of many nationalities with the blood of Chinese, Japanese, Indians, Malays, Ceylonese, Indonesians, Filipinos, Polynesians, Melanesians, Portuguese and the mainland Aboriginal in their veins. Amid this conglomeration are the Torres Strait Islanders with their vitality and joy in life that is the envy of newcomers to the straits.

On the islands and mainland Queensland, Torres Strait Islanders number about 6,000 in all. They are not a poor people and are law abiding citizens. Many live in European type houses surrounded by neat gardens. Quite large luggers are owned by families on T.I. who staff the ships and share the profits accrued from diving for pearl and trochus shell for export. The Torres Strait Islanders are not "free" citizens. Their wages are paid into the account of the Department of Native Affairs which issues money from the earner's income.

I noticed that direct payments were made to mothers still in hospital with new born babies and was often intrigued at seeing officers from the Department of Native Affairs going about their jobs, in pairs, and with briefcases in hand. Child endowment payments were made to mothers on the birth of the child. Usually the coloured mother showed little interest in the policy and shook her head in negative response to the offer of money.

Many Torres Strait Island couples enjoy Church blessing on their union; others, as in the past, disregard the Church's ceremony of marriage.

Islanders seem to have no moral background as we know it and illegitimacy carries no stigma. Girls with three or more children showed no embarrassment in stating "single"

TOP LEFT:The author with children from the Hammond Island Settlement, Torres Strait, Queensland. The island, protected by government and church, has earned the name "Island For Children." TOP RIGHT: These charming Torres Strait Islanders work as domestics at the Thursday Island General Hospital. These girls are excellent workers, always cheerful and efficient. BOTTOM: A proud mother and grandmother lovingly admire the latest addition to the family

when asked their marital status for clinic record. It was not unusual for the mother of the girl to stand in the way of a regular union if she wanted to hold on to her daughter's services in the home and benefit from fortnightly child endowment payments.

"Mother does not want me to get married," explained a handsome girl, mother of two children.

When I questioned another girl bringing her fourth baby to the Clinic, she replied airily, "Me engaged, not married!"

Torres Strait Island babies are breast fed for the first year of life with selected soft foods being introduced at varying months till the beginning of the second year. The one year old is encouraged to eat the same native foodstuffs as its parents. These children seldom suffered from dietary disorders or infantile rashes.

There was little sale for aperients with coconut milk serving as a laxative. Contrary to its customary use, paraffin oil was sold locally as a hairdressing product.

Island mothers frequently named their offspring after the nurse or doctor who attended them at the confinement and, not infrequently, gave their children the name of a comparative stranger. I recall a mother wanting a name for her new born, six pound boy. She had come from a mission station on the mainland to have her baby at the T.I. Hospital.

"Call him William," I volunteered on the spur of the moment.

"Why that name?"

"After the Reverend William McKenzie of Aurukun Mission on the gulf," I replied.

She promptly acquiesced and the baby was named William for life.

Old Testament names were popular for boys—Joseph, Jeremiah, Moses, Samuel, and Jacob. So were the modern names of Larry, Lester, and Brian. Full names took unexpected turns so that Paul Tom, Barney Barney, and Tamwoy Jack emerged. Double names such as Mairu Mairu sounded strangely on the European ear.

Handling several babies on a normal clinic day, weighing

Simon is reputed to be the oldest man on Thursday Island and probably of the whole Torres Straits. He is a permanent resident of the General Hospital, which is situated on a spectacular promontory called Hospital Point in the south-western section of the town. The Hospital can accommodate 200 patients

them on the table scales, and examining their naked bodies for physical defects, I quickly formed the opinion that Torres Strait babies are unique and those of other races, at the time, seemed to pall in significance. These babies seemed so wise from the beginning, and enjoyed maximum freedom of movement from the earliest age. They contradicted normal milestones of development to a surprising degree. At three months, looking like young Amazons, they even attempted to stand erect on bare feet.

I was struck too by the natural way they responded to music; eyes lit up at the sound and hands moved in time with the beat. Artificially fed infants demanded twice as much milk as the text books instructed for weight and age. One boy of five weeks whose mother had tuberculosis was satisfied with nothing less than the quantity and strength adequate for a six months old child.

I often heard a mother remark proudly, "'im turn over on belly," if the baby was under three months of age. Even fathers were eager to tell of their offspring's prowess in this direction. "'im clever fella my son. 'im turn over on belly, crawl to mudder in kitchen. Talk my lingo, too," one of them said.

Yes, the children did extraordinary things from the earliest age. I recall a three weeks old baby lying quietly on the clinic scales, and as I stood observing her, a breathtaking smile flashed across the face to disappear for a moment and then come again. It was as if a ray of sunshine had flashed across a dark sky to leave behind a lasting memory of unexpected joy, a stirring of peculiar emotion in the heart.

If clinic attendance never achieved anything but the self-imposed discipline of mothers presenting themselves regularly and neatly dressed with their young, proudly displayed in nylon or cotton garments, it was worthwhile. It seemed almost a ritual for a new baby to wear cream woollen bonnet and bootees when they were first brought to the clinic. I warned against the habit but it continued and it seemed that even on the hottest afternoon, the infant suffered no discomfort or ill effects from the wearing of

24

these unnecessary articles of clothing. Children up to five years attended the Child Welfare clinics and toddlers appeared dressed in gay sunsuits with jaunty sailor or jockey caps—added for effect rather than for protection.

They were somewhat prone to small tropical sores on exposed skin areas but these required no further treatment than application of Gentian Violet, a purple-coloured, antiseptic healing lotion which I had used with excellent results in other tropical areas.

When a six months old baby boy, Andrew Namok, became northern zone winner in the Queensland Centenary Quest, the Torres Strait Islanders were jubilant. Lady Cilento, doctor and child specialist, headed a panel of judges.

When I enrolled him, on behalf of his mother, in the under twelve months section, Andrew was a lively, engaging child, twenty-two pounds and still being breast fed. He was the northernmost finalist and the only coloured child in the quest.

We flew from Thursday Island to Brisbane and Andrew, in primrose silk suit with matching beret, socks, and sandals, had gathered an appreciative audience as soon as the aircraft left Horn Island. The colour of his outfit was a perfect foil to his large, brown eyes and shining skin.

At the judging he stood alone on bare feet for the first time, aged six and a half months, and one newspaper headlined Lady Cilento's announcement:"Chocolate Baby Captures Their Hearts."

I quote further: "Andrew is a perfect baby. He has everything. It is very appropriate in this centenary year to see an original Queenslander in the finals of the quest."

The surnames of many well-known Torres Strait Island families appeared on record cards at the clinic. And none was more highly respected than "Mosby", a name that originated last century when Edward Mosby, a sailor from Boston, U.S.A., deserted his ship in the Torres Straits and went to York Island. He settled among kindly Islanders, married a local girl, reared a family and became known far and wide as "Yankee Ned".

His descendants still live on York Island and some on T.I. where they are active members of the Anglican Church, a great grandson being ordained priest in an impressive cathedral ceremony in 1959.

An invitation was received that year, through Miss Lilian Schoedler, an American visitor on a goodwill tour of the Straits. It came from the mayor of Boston and requested that the great grandson of Yankee Ned visit the States and represent Yankee Ned's family as guest of the city from which he came. To my knowledge, the journey never eventuated.

5

HORN ISLAND

HORN ISLAND, ABOUT TWENTY square miles in area, lies
fifteen miles north-west of Cape York in Queensland.

An important present day adjunct to Thursday Island,
it was originally the haunt of primitive natives. It takes its
name from Horned Hill which Matthew Flinders, in 1803,
described as "forming something like two horns at the
top". In approaching from the north-west he first thought
that the land was part of Prince of Wales Island. The two
islands are in fact separated only by a very narrow channel.

History records that he anchored for the night under the
"queer shaped hill". Next morning his exploring party
landed on the island, discovered fresh water by digging in
a hollow, and saw trees bearing a harsh, astringent fruit
resembling a plum. It was probably a species of the indigenous wongai tree which exists there today.

Some of the early explorers reported seeing burial places
but no inhabitants. Others described how they avoided
shooting at night for fear of disturbing the natives which
they had every reason to believe were not far distant.
Twelve years before Matthew Flinders, Captain Edwards

arrived at Horn Island in the *Pandora* and wrote about wild beasts filling the woods at night with hideous growling of wolves. In his book, Robert Jack claimed this early reference to be the first mention of the dingo as an indigenous animal of the Straits. Nowadays it is generally believed that the dingo has evolved from the Asiatic wolf or the Indian wild dog and the earlier theory of the dingo being indigenous has been largely discredited by researchers.

Gold was discovered on the island in 1894 and the area was proclaimed a goldfield. Prospectors and syndicates carried out reefing operations and a Company was formed. From an opencut mine thirty feet deep ore was obtained from what was believed to be the famous "Welcome Stranger" reef. In those days as many as twenty-seven mines were operating on Horn Island. A flourishing, temporary settlement sprang up and constant trafficking began between Horn Island and Thursday Island.

Veteran miner Bill Franks, remarkably fit for his eighty years, and a tall, lean man with tanned, weatherbeaten skin, recalled those mining days. In 1960 he became surveyor to a Thursday Island building contractor interested in an old mining site on Horn Island.

"I was living in retirement down south. My wife said I was too old to start again, but I guess it was the gold fever got me again," he explained.

He went to Thursday Island first in 1905 with the first batch of militia troops from New South Wales that had been sent to aid the Queensland Garrison. There was no doubt that he had enjoyed those early days.

"There were about 150 men in the garrison, 800 whites and about as many Japs in the town; some Geisha girls too," he mused. "The Orientals lived in a boarding house settlement called 'Yokohama' and as well as a chemist shop there were six pubs and the two-storied premises of the Fresh Food and Ice Company. Beer was tuppence a pint—a bloke could get drunk on two bob! Fortunes were made in the pearling industry and there were so many sovereigns about that blokes used the gold coins as coat buttons and had them made into watch chains."

28

After his discharge from the Army, Bill worked at a gold mine on Horn Island and later took up building and painting on T.I. He married the daughter of a local sailmaker but the gold fever got him again and from 1911 to 1921 he looked for gold on the island, built a house, and raised a family of five boys and a girl.

Speaking of present day medical and other social benefits, Bill grimly remarked, "In those days there was nothing. Not even child endowment for the white people."

He ran a blacksmith's shop on T.I. for three years, employed five men, called the business the "Torres Strait General Repair Company" and tackled everything from shoeing horses, plumbing, and carpentering.

On leaving the Straits in 1924, he never expected to return, but he went back after forty years.

"The local legend says he who eats of the Wongai tree will return to the Island—and I ate it," he added.

That was Bill Franks. A grand old story teller.

After the gold mining operations the hills of Horn Island were claimed by Malayans and Filipinos who built houses, grew vegetables, paw paw fruit, bananas and pineapples.

A well-known pearl buyer visiting the Straits after thirty years recollected that in those days it was possible to buy a bunch of bananas nearly a foot long for one shilling and sixpence. He complained that at the time he spoke he would pay nearly that much for one banana.

The Asiatics living on Horn Island made a very potent alcoholic beverage from small coconut palms growing in abundance on the island. They cut at the base of the flowers at certain stages of growth, fixed a hollow tube, such as a length of bamboo, to the base and allowed the liquid from the flower to drip into a bottle or jar placed in position beneath the tube. In this way, over a period of six weeks a quantity of sweet juice, intended by nature for the making of coconuts, was collected and mixed with water. The result was a cider-like, potent drink.

If allowed to stand for three days the juice became a wonderful yeast for the making of bread. When distilled and used as a beverage, the effects from the drink were said to be worse than those brought on by methylated spirits. It was called "tuba" by the Islanders. I gathered that its impact on the nervous system was almost instantaneous. It made men so wobbly on the legs they could not stand up. Tuba was a popular drink but eventually the brewing of coconut flower juice was declared illegal by the government.

Before the second World War aircraft occasionally landed on the commercial airstrip on the south-western end of the island, and prior to Japan's entry into the war in 1942, bomber fighter planes were housed there.

The bitter conflict in Europe made Horn Island an internationally known war establishment with the island becoming strategically important in the defence of Australia. When war came to Europe in 1939, international authorities decided to enlarge the northernmost airfield in Australia. The Queensland government was responsible for the project and a well-known English engineer, Mr Fred Lord, was put in charge of construction. The Horn Island airfield became the staging strip for planes from Morotai and from Lae.

Before the Coral Sea Battle lifted the threat of invasion from the north Queensland coast, hundreds of Australians, and later American airmen, were held on Horn Island in readiness for Japanese raiders who made the area a regular place of call.

The first Japanese aircraft to be shot down by the Allies landed on near-by Hammond Island. It is said Thursday Island escaped attack only because a revered Japanese princess lay buried in the local cemetery. No one appeared to know the exact site of her grave.

In March 1942, fortunately after all civilians had been evacuated, Japanese raiders flew over the Straits and dropped nearly two hundred bombs. At this time Horn Islanders became accustomed to the sight of Mitchells, Kittyhawks, American Beauforts, Flying Fortresses, and other types of aircraft using the Straits. They then saw their island become the staging camp for allied airmen on the way north and south. It was the base for air raids on

Salamaua, Rabaul, and Lae. There were tragic wartime accidents — one American plane was reported to have struck ground, burst into flames, and left only one survivor from the crew and skilled technical specialists it carried.

Throughout its turbulent wartime history, Horn Island received many scars and collected many souvenirs. Six months after the Coral Sea Battle ended, lifebelts, cartridges, water bottles, and odds and ends of Japanese equipment were flung up on its shores. The wartime legacy to the island included the enlarged airfield, a huge disused dam, good roads, and the remains of a radar station. Peacetime natives uncovered a bomb within two miles of the airstrip and the R.A.A.F. disposal experts exploded four high-explosive bombs. Scattered forty-gallon petrol drums litter the near-by bush and the wrecks of planes can be seen in the water at low tide. Civilians with financial interests in the Strait lost heavily and among them was Geodon Vidgen from an old Somerset family. Before the war he bred cattle on Horn Island and managed a butcher's shop on T.I. With some bitterness he aired his grievance of wartime losses: "When top American personnel flew in looking for a possible defence site on Horn Island, the pilots swooped in for landings and killed a lot of my cattle. The government authorities gave only five pounds a head for cattle they killed. Those cattle were really good beasts and worth much more."

With no dairy herds on Horn Island and no fresh milk former residents now living on T.I. recall the days of the horse and cart outfit and the "Milk-Oh! Milk-Oh!"

At the end of the war buildings and equipment were sold at disposal sales and soon afterwards Horn Island became deserted.

It entered into the last and present phase in 1946 with the arrival of natives from Kubin Village on Moa Island. Some of those who came had been employed by the Department of Civil Aviation during the war, had liked the locality, and when the island was no longer a war area, brought their families to live there. With negroid features and darker skin they were more like mainland Aborigines than

Torres Strait Islanders. Their forebears were the men of the Muralug tribe which formerly occupied Prince of Wales Island. It was a tribe noted for savagery.

These nomadic islanders, in the nature of events and movements over the years, practically lost their tribal identity and were referred to as "Horn Islanders".

They used the remains of army huts, bush timber, and wartime scraps to build the temporary crude dwellings, lasting to this day, on a cleared site beyond the palm-clad shore. The primitive settlement, with gloomy shelters almost devoid of furniture, was the home of about one hundred and twenty men, women, and children.

The Horn Islanders show no inclination to cultivate the soil or go on further walkabout; rather than return to their official village on Moa Island they have chosen to live in the shelters and enjoy their proximity to Thursday Island.

The most important person on the settlement was the school teacher, Willie Namie, who was employed by the Department of Native Affairs. He taught thirty children whose ages ranged from six to fourteen years. Speaking and writing fair English, he cheerfully fulfilled a variety of community roles.

Willie Namie was gentle in manner and striking in appearance. He had smoke-black skin, a massive chest and bull neck that reminded one of a powerful wrestler. It was something to see him striding along on his broad, flat feet with the easy grace of a panther. He was a conspicuous figure in bright red lava lava which reached nearly to his ankles, and arranged with bunches of fold in front to suit his heavy figure. His chest bulged in the tight-fitting white singlet. Willie was always a pleasant, able assistant when I visited the settlement to check the health of the children. They sometimes had small, ugly sores on limbs, defective teeth, and lice-ridden hair.

For each of my visits children stood grouped together in front of the schoolhouse and as I approached Willie led them in unison with the greeting, "Good Morning Sister". He formed the children into queues, called names from clinic cards, pacified frightened toddlers, and generally kept law and order.

Although living in slum-like conditions, Horn Islanders appeared adequately fed; some of the men worked in near-by T.I. and people spent a lot of their time fishing and swimming. Sardines abound in the surrounding waters, supplying good bait for catching the nutritious white fish, barramundi, and king fish. All excellent food.

As seen around Aboriginal camps in outback Australia, skinny, yelping dogs roamed the settlement. The only other kind of animal I encountered was a coarse-haired black pig described by Willie as a "pet". It was not the only one, he assured me; there were pet snakes and also a few goats.

Uncultivated banana palms and low spreading melon bushes provided welcome addition to the people's diet.

At the conclusion of clinic duties Willie voluntarily accompanied me to the jetty to await the government motor launch scheduled to pick up aircraft passengers for T.I.

Willie told me that he was forty-six years old and that he had been teaching for six years. His mother was born on Prince of Wales and he was born on Moa. He was top boy at the Church of England Mission School on Moa Island. For twenty years he had worked on luggers, learnt music from "the white man" and remembered the words of their songs. He began studies at the theological college to become a priest but became ill and did not finish the course. It seemed that he then learned to sing and act in concerts on Palm Island Aboriginal Settlement in north Queensland. Proud of his position on the island he voiced his displeasure over parents who took their children camping instead of sending them to the school house each day. "They should think first of the children's education for future," he said earnestly.

Another character who lived on Horn Island for some years was "Rattler Tom". His age was uncertain although it was generally known that he was born on the British warship H.M.S. *Rattlesnake* and that he was the last surviving member of the Muralug tribe.

About the middle of the last century the H.M.S. *Rattle-snake* accompanied Kennedy on his ill-fated expedition from Sydney. The ship later played a dramatic part in the rescue of the Scottish woman, Barbara Thompson, sole survivor of the shipwreck in the Torres Strait. When on a visit to T.I. a few years ago, Rattler Tom collapsed and he died a few days later in the general hospital.

On one occasion when I was delayed on the settlement and Willie had taken me to the jetty, we saw the launch moving into the distance. "Look! Launch she go!" he shouted, and as dismayed and excited as a forlorn castaway of fiction, he raced to the top of a near-by sandy rise above the beach. He flung off his lava lava and as if fanning a fainting person, waved the garment in the direction of the speeding vessel. I remained unharmed and safe until rescued later in the day. Previously as a foreigner I would have been put to death.

Horn Islanders are accustomed now to the sight of modern aircraft approaching or departing from the near-by aerodrome and quickly detected different engine sounds. "That not passenger plane, that survey plane," Willie would comment in a knowledgeable way as aircraft flew overhead while we walked to the jetty and I talked of the twice-weekly passenger plane.

In one of the mangrove swamps lie the remains of a Lockheed Hudson plane which crashed on 1 July 1957. It had been engaged in a photographic survey. Eight minutes after taking off from the Horn Island airfield, on the return flight to Weipa, the plane crashed on a jagged coral beach with the loss of the pilot and the five passengers aboard. Among the dead was the founder of the Queensland Aero Club and the director of Mitchell Aerial Services Pty Ltd, Mr William Mitchell. Photographic equipment ruined in the crash was valued at 20,000 dollars.

All that the well dressed southern visitor to the Strait usually sees of Horn Island is the austere airport building, virgin forest lining the bus route, and glimpses of crude native dwellings reminiscent of a Singapore slum. They see nothing of the old mine sites at the other end of the island where picturesque ghost gums and towering coconut palms offset the harshness of former industrial activity.

With complete absence of fear, Horn Islanders swim almost before they can walk. If they are lucky, visitors might see the glistening bodies of young children shooting through the water like otters, or bobbing up and down like turtles near the jetty. And before boarding the launch for T.I. they might even get a delightful camera shot to remind them of a fleeting glimpse of life near Australia's most northern airfield.

6

BEWARE OF THE WONGAI

THE LONE WONGAI TREE growing in beach sand in front of the Federal Hotel was planted by the father of the oldest resident, now over eighty years of age, Miss Maggie McNulty. She was one of the most pleasantly informed people I met in T.I.

Maggie McNulty grew up surrounded by the song and legend of the wongai tree which, at one time, was worshipped as a god. Nowadays people still say: "Eat of the wongai tree and you will return to T.I." The nut-like fruit-bearing tree with the dark foliage is indigenous to the Torres Strait but it is said to be found growing in Fiji. It is protected by law. Children, especially, love the small, round fruit that falls to the ground when ripe. To me the fruit was tasteless and I thought it resembled a dry date. I hope to return to T.I. one day, and residents have no doubt that I am bound to their coral straits forever.

The tree in front of the hotel is sharply bent and misshapen. Thursday Islanders say it turned away from a coconut tree growing near the roots. "Those trees no like it other," they commented.

Some years ago the McNulty family erected a guard around the tree to prevent root damage. From the verandah of the Federal Hotel, where she now sits most of the day, Miss McNulty guards the family relic.

Words describing the alleged hypnotic spell of the wongai tree have been put to music, and the song is a popular number at local concerts and farewells, on radio, and at reunions in Brisbane.

As visitors to T.I. distinguished people in show business appear to be legion. There was Bert Bayley of "On Our Selection" fame; Howard Vernon, the celebrated singer of J. C. Williamson's company; and Dame Nordica, renowned American singer of a distant era.

Dame Nordica became a patient in the local hospital and was so pleased with the treatment received that she left the institution a handsome donation. She died later in Java.

When Sir Harry Lauder and Company came ashore in the 1920s, a wag on the wharf called to the great Scottish comedian, "How about a song, Harry?" The party left their signatures in the hotel Visitors Book.

The book, tatty with age and use, is a storehouse of distinguished personal signatures, of men famous in science, politics, naval and military affairs, medicine, and the entertainments. Attached to it is the newspaper cuttings book dating back seventy years, with illustrations and descriptions of personalities, places, anecdotes, and stirring events from Thursday Island's past.

Miss Gladys Moncrieff, the Bundaberg girl who became "Our Glad" to thousands, came to T.I. as a girl of seventeen or eighteen. She sang at the local town hall which was packed for the occasion.

In Thursday Island's heyday the Wirths and Bullens circuses thought it worthwhile to bring their heavy equipment and menagerie ashore. Miss McNulty told how Wirths broke a long sea voyage to spend two days on the Island and made a profit of $500. Lions were not allowed ashore but the monkeys and elephants went. She said that as a child her favourite show had been the midgets, Mr and Mrs Tom

Thumb. The hair-raising act of a Japanese woman walking barefoot on a shining, open sword was second in her estimation.

The merry-go-round was always the first choice of children but at a shilling a round it was not cheap entertainment.

The Federal Hotel carried "Under Vice Regal Patronage" after Sir Matthew Nathen had lunch there. He was on his way to London by ship on completion of his term of service as Governor of Queensland.

Sir Matthew Nathan was a friend and admirer of the Country Women's Association, a great Australian institution. One of his last official acts in Australia was to form a branch of the Association on Thursday Island. Christmas greetings assuring the branch of his continued interest were received from him annually up to the time of his death.

Among well-known writers who left and some who returned are Jack London and Guy Boothby, authors of the long forgotten best sellers *Beautiful White Devil* and *The Marriage of Esther*.

One of the most popular literary tourists to holiday on the island was Miss Philipa Bridges, sister of Sir Thomas Bridges, famous politician and soldier. Unassuming and friendly, she entered into the life of the people and was quite enchanted with the island.

Another well-known writer, Beatrice Grimshaw, talked to members of the Royal Geographical Society during a visit to T.I. from New Guinea.

Most famous of them all, Somerset Maugham, put up at the hotel with his secretary in 1916. An old resident remembered him complaining about the lack of fresh fruit on the breakfast table.

Lord Northcliffe was another visitor, and in 1946 Lady Bisset, wife of Commander Bisset of the *Queen Mary*, arrived in T.I. from Brisbane in the old passenger steamship *Wandana*.

In the newspaper cuttings book is a one page copy of the *Horn Herald* dated 12 May 1943, "Printed And Published With Apologies From The Editor On Magazine Hill, Horn

TOP: Pearling divers discuss their work prior to sailing to the largest oyster shell beds in the world. The lustrous mother-of-pearl lining of these shells provides employment for many Thursday Islanders. BOTTOM: The pearl shells are being unloaded from the trawler and will soon be exported for the making of buttons, studs, and novelties

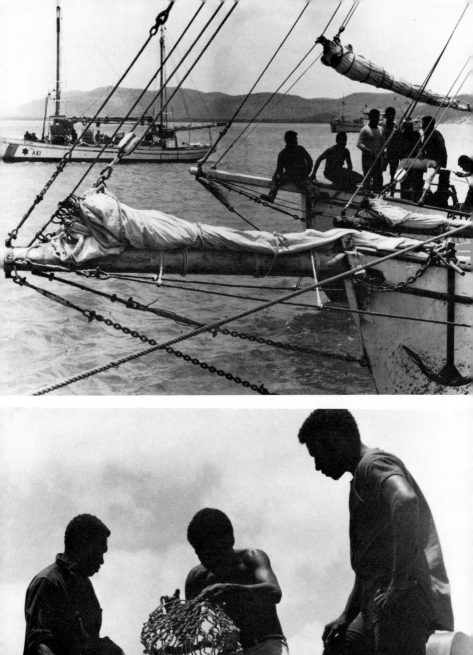

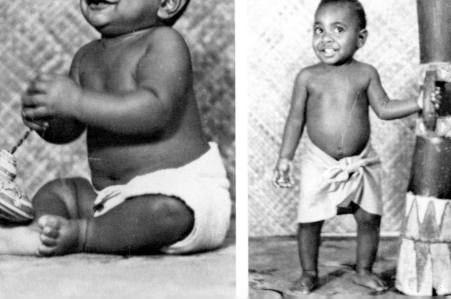

Island." The motto of this small wartime newspaper was "Tomorrow's news today if not sooner."

The page carried paragraphs of B.B.C. news, a vivid account of the latest air raid on Darwin, and an advertisement for the T.I. cinema film at that time, *High, Wide and Handsome*. The advertisement stated that five short feature films were to be shown.

No visitor loved T.I. more than Professor Archibald Watson, M.D., F.R.C.S., L.S.M., Professor Emeritus of the Adelaide University. He has been described as the "greatest anatomist Australia ever produced". Some of the interesting newspaper cuttings tell of his distinguished career. After his retirement Professor Watson lived on Thursday Island for nearly five years. It was an outstanding example of the fascination a small, tropical island can exert on a man.

A familiar and well-loved figure around the waterfront, he was usually seen carrying a fishing rod, and was always ready to stop and entertain with his stories. He would dissect fish, sea snake, or turtle and explain their workings to delighted Islanders.

At the age of eighty-seven he was riding a motorcycle around the Island streets and he died at the age of ninety-one in the local hospital. He was one visitor to whom the legend of the Wongai tree did not apply. Once there he never left the island for any length of time. He was buried on a hill site overlooking the blue waters of the Strait.

"Just the place Proffy would love," one of his friends said. His epitaph was "He Loved His Fellow Man".

Horn Island made front page news in 1960 with the arrival of Michael Fomenko. Son of a Sydney school teacher, and aged twenty-nine years, he had cut himself off from civilisation because he wanted to. Locals named him Tarzan.

In probably the longest small boat journey in Australian history, since Bass and Flinders went south from Sydney in the *Tom Thumb*, Michael Fomenko sailed his fifteen-footer, dug-out canoe from Cairns to the Torres Strait.

Months after he had been feared lost Fomenko weighted

TOP: Young people from Badu relax after work. The Torres Strait Islanders are a distinct race, related more to the Papuans than the mainland Aborigines. BOTTOM LEFT: Andrew Namok at six and a half months. He was the northern zone winner in the Queensland Centenary Quest. He weighed twenty-two pounds and was still breast-fed. BOTTOM RIGHT: Torres Strait Islanders are unique in that they contradict normal milestones of development to a surprising degree. At three months, looking like young Amazons, they attempt to stand erect

his roughly hewn craft in a mangrove swamp on Horn Island. Next day he was discovered by a party of Horn Islanders who informed the policeman at Thursday Island.

In the days that followed, T.I. buzzed with excitement whenever the dishevelled Tarzan appeared to purchase flour, tea, sugar, and other commodities necessary to continue his proposed journey to the Solomon Islands. Tied up near the wharf, his primitive canoe with mangrove wood mast, crude outrigging, and cotton-wool stabilisers was viewed both with amazement and derision by curious onlookers. One voiced the thoughts of others with, "I wouldn't go five miles in that thing." His voice carried surprise and disgust.

The canoe contained plastic buoys for carrying fresh water, car tubes for the storing of sugar and flour, crude spears for the hunting of wild game, and a fish net for holding copra.

Michael Fomenko travelled along the Queensland coast sitting at the stern of his canoe and using a broken-off paddle to move along. He was probably the only man to sail the entire Queensland coast in this way.

He said he was never very far from the beach, that he stopped each night to make camp, and stayed when necessary to hunt for food. His diet consisted of oysters, wild fowl, fish, and crocodiles which were killed with the big knife he wore at his waist.

He got on well with the friendly Horn Islanders, sharing their humble dwellings, going on walkabout through the bush, and catching fish off the jetty for breakfast each morning as was their habit.

Doctors at the T.I. Hospital were interested in the close proximity of the lone voyager, hoping to give him a full physical examination to assess the effects of his spartan way of life. No proffered advice given by well-wishers could induce the rank individualist to report to the hospital. He claimed he was fit and well, ignoring the professional opinion that he should be inoculated against tropical diseases before proceeding farther.

When I met him suddenly one Horn Island clinic day I

did my best to persuade him but without result. In appearance he resembled the present day hippie. Tall, lean, barefooted, with long hair reaching almost to his shoulders, face covered with thick beard, he wore only a pair of tattered khaki trousers. A magnificent conch shell, a gift of the Horn Islanders, hung on his deeply tanned chest. He had promised to wear it permanently.

At official level in T.I. Michael Fomenko refused the free air ticket to Sydney and seemed unmoved by the thousand dollars offered for his life story.

John Caldwell, author of *Desperate Voyage*, suggested that Fomenko go on to Darwin with him in his launch, *Outward Bound*, that had anchored for a few days in the T.I. harbour. Fomenko turned down the offer as he had made up his mind to sail to the Solomon Islands in his rough canoe. But to the delight of the skipper he did visit the boat and John Caldwell got a first-hand scoop story of the nine day wonder for a Sydney newspaper.

In 1960 Frank Nicklin, who was premier of Queensland at that time, paid an official visit to T.I. His late aunt, Miss Alice Nicklin, was saved from the wreck of the *Quetta* when she was nineteen years old and the premier officially named an island off the southern end of Mount Adolphus after her.

Thursday Island's rambling hilltop cemetery overlooking Aplin Pass records local history dating back to 1875 with the burial of a man named Smyth whose son became first town clerk of the island community. Biblical texts and Christian symbols on the tombstones give eloquent testimony to the influence of Christianity in the last century.

On the highest hill a slim, grey stone obelisk rises like Cleopatra's Needle. The broad base is inscribed:

Sacred to the Memory of John Douglas. Born March 5th, 1828. Died July 3rd, 1905
Premier of Queensland, 1877-1888
Special Commissioner British New Guinea 1886
Government Resident Thursday Island 1885-1886-1904
"Write Me As A Man Who Loved His Fellow Man."

An imposing memorial to another who earned the same epitaph, Professor Watson, stands near-by.

In one corner of the cemetery Japanese characters at the top of small white posts mark multiple graves of heroes of the sea, the intrepid Japanese pearl divers. Traditional glass-domed artificial flowers, cups, empty wine glasses, forks and spoons are placed on non-European graves.

Many years after a death in the family the Blessing of the Stone is held. Relatives and friends of the deceased, dressed in their best, brightest clothes, walk in slow procession through the cemetery, singing and chanting, until they reach the graveside. The new tombstone, shrouded in beautiful and costly materials, is a spectacular sight amid the drabness of surrounding graves. A priest unveils and blesses the stone in a solemn and dignified ceremony and later in the day energy is spent in traditional feasting and dancing.

I consider Torres Strait Islanders to be among the happiest people in the world; they are well cared for by a benevolent government and are unimpressed with financial involvement and material possessions. I cannot recall one true islander child who suffered from neglect or malnutrition. They are a sentimental people, loving feasting, dancing, and the music of their culture. They have the brightest smiles and are easily aroused to infectious laughter.

Singing is a way of life and an integral part of their religion. At the convent school in T.I., where music is taught by the nuns, Torres Strait Island children excel in music competitions held among children throughout Queensland for state awards. The popular, sentimental song, "T.I. My Beautiful Home," expresses simply their love of the islands. Now almost a national song, it was sung first in the 1940s. As a song of farewell, it echoed from the deck of a passenger ship as T.I. boys, enlisted in the Armed Services, sailed away from their home for the first time. Since then it has been sung by flower-decked crowds gathered on the wharf to farewell the monthly passenger ship carrying holiday-makers and visitors to and from this idyllic South Sea Island.

T.I. My Beautiful Home,
The place where I was born,
Where the sun and the moon they shine
   To make me longing for home.

   Take me across the sea,
   Over the deep blue sea,
   Darling, won't you take me,
      Back to my home, T.I.?

T.I. My Beautiful Home,
      Tis *my* home, sweet home,
      I'll be there forever
Till the sun is sinking farewell
      T.I., My Beautiful Home.

7

ENCHANTED ISLAND

PEOPLE ON T.I. GO BOATING on Sundays and plan a cruise in much the same way as city folk a trip to the seaside or weekend motoring. Thursday Islanders prefer to go off to uninhabited islands. They say that the air is fresher there than in the town of T.I. Getting away from it all sounded rather strange to a newcomer from down south where the hemmed-in feeling, brought on by bustling streets and crowded shops, made any island in the Pacific seem the fulfilment of a Utopian dream.

Beautiful, peaceful Friday Island is an escapist's place. It has what other islands have not; it is handy to T.I., with a safe harbour all year round; water in the channel is perpetually calm and untouched by the vagaries of tropical winds and storms. On the south-west end of the island a spectacular pearly sandbank, two and a half miles wide, runs for nine miles and most of it is uncovered at low tide.

The native name for the island is *Gugula*. Probably it was christened Friday for the day on which it was discovered. Tuesday and Wednesday Islands were named in the early days by Captain Bligh on his way to the open seas after the mutiny of the *Bounty*. History emphatically records that he could not have named Thursday or Friday Islands, and who named Friday Island is not clear. At least one historian gives the credit of naming Friday Island to Captain Parker-King (later Rear-Admiral) who was in the area in 1848, but the name Friday Island does not appear on Captain Parker's charts.

Friday Island for me was the enchanted island; a beautiful place, rich in local history, colour, and mystery and somehow evocative of the adventures of Robinson Crusoe. Perhaps it was the name, reminiscent of Man Friday and also reminding me of a beloved dog I adopted when I was nursing in Labrador. I called him Friday and on the sunlit beaches of Friday Island would remember him swimming in the icy seas off the stony coast of Labrador.

Friday Island is one mile in length and lies two miles south-west of T.I. It is separated from Prince of Wales Island by a channel five hundred feet wide.

Prettily timbered with evergreen casuarinas, wild fig, wongai, and almond trees—the most magnificent specimens I have seen anywhere in the tropics—the island has fine, good-looking beaches with low sand dunes making it an ideal site for picnics, barbecues, and weekend camping. In parts the area has the startling appearance of a white sandy desert with long rolling dunes bare of vegetation reminding me of the sweeping sand hill country in Central Australia.

The beaches on Friday Island are the laying grounds for the green turtle. It makes its egg-laying pilgrimages up the beach and then disappears again. When the eggs hatch, the young scramble across the sands until their flippers find the water and their natural home.

Flocks of birds fly overhead wheeling their way across the sky. The Torres Strait is the annual route of all migratory birds; some go further north to New Guinea and some fly south. Large convoys of birds go thousands of miles to Siberia and elsewhere in northern Europe about April each year. They rest in the northern hemisphere during summer and return to Australia and the Torres Strait about October each year. I first watched a large flock of these migratory birds soaring and wheeling in the sky above the blue waters of Friday Island. Commonly called sea birds, they had large, white wings and were probably members of the wader bird family of which there are many known species.

Friday Island was once the meeting place for friendly tribes who came from their own islands in wooden dug-out canoes for primitive ceremonies.

The geographical formation of the Torres Strait Islands is very ancient. Most were inhabited by savages and it is not difficult to imagine many of the dramas and rituals being enacted with feasting and dancing on the ceremonial ground, a large, treeless, circular area, at the south-western end of Friday Island. Even today remnants of the past remain. I practically walked over history one day when ambling along the foreshore. Fine sand and fragmentary substance spread like geographical strata beneath my feet. My knowledgeable companion pointed it out as the remains of an ancient kitchen midden, feeding ground of the Stone Age people. I was fascinated with the unexpected discovery; a myriad of tiny particles of sea shell mixed with fine sand revealing entirely different native living to that seen on the mainland where heaps of discarded mussel shells marked the temporary eating places of the nomadic Aboriginal. It seemed that, in comparison, the Torres Strait primitive man used the same eating site, generation after generation, living not only on turtle and dugong wrested from the sea, but upon the soft molluscs of countless small sea shells.

This island midden, which we were lucky to find, may have been hidden in the sand for hundreds of years. As I left the historical site I wondered with melancholy interest if fragments of human bones, discarded after ancient cannibal feasts, also lay beneath the surface area of this ancient rubbish heap.

After the introduction of white civilisation, human skeletons and bones were found on the island at high water mark beneath the sand. In the early days the heathen islanders usually murdered castaways without question, regarding them as enemies. At times it seemed as if the serene, tropical atmosphere of Friday Island was filled with the unheeded cries of those who met violent deaths in terrible massacres.

Typical of the many ships wrecked in this area whose crews met their fates at the hands of cannibals was the *Sapphire* which left Gladstone in Queensland for Calcutta in 1857. She was wrecked in the Torres Strait near the entrance of Raine Island, scene of many earlier wrecks. The crew took to the boats but unwisely called at Friday Island, where natives attacked and killed all the men in the captain's boat.

Sailing Directions for the Torres Strait was first published five years after this happening. In the first edition of this publication voyagers were warned to be on their guard at all times against the treachery of natives when trading, going ashore at different islands, watering their ships, or collecting wood. Despite warnings white men still ventured into dangerous areas and met with murder. One newspaper printed "the worst massacre ever heard of," and to this day the fate of the trading vessel *Sperwer* still hangs over Friday Island. Torres Strait Islanders, recalling the grim events, refuse to stay overnight on Friday Island.

Captain Gascoigne, skipper of the *Sperwer*, left Melbourne in 1869 bound for New Guinea with his twelve-year-old son and a crew that was either Malayan or Chinese. There were seventeen in all. He planned to stay a while in the Torres Straits, his ship being the first to leave a southern port to work pearl in the Straits. It was a dangerous undertaking, for in addition to the savage reputation of the Islanders and the treacherous northern waters, there were no lights or beacons to warn of navigational danger. These were not installed until the 1870s.

Captain Gascoigne must have been a sterling seaman. He navigated a thousand miles through the coral traps of the Great Barrier Reef without calling in at Somerset on Cape York, then a four-year-old haven for ships passing that way. His lonely voyage ended when he dropped anchor off

Friday Island, apparently deserted but in fact far more threatening than any other of the dangers he had passed.

The captain's son and most of the crew went ashore at sunset for food and water. When the party was out of sight, a savage tribe from Prince of Wales Island stole along in canoes, murdered Captain Gascoigne and the two members of the crew aboard at the time, and later, in a terrible carnage, ambushed the unsuspecting shore party and murdered the lot.

News of the *Sperwer*'s fate reached Somerset several weeks after the massacre and Captain Gascoigne's log book, clothing, and ship's gear were found on Prince of Wales Island. The government avenged the *Sperwer* murders by a grim, punitive expedition that forced the natives into a cul-de-sac so that there was no hope of escape. The largest island in the Torres Strait, Prince of Wales Island, was almost depopulated by the mass shooting that took place.

The action gave rise to fears and controversy among earnest-thinking people who, for years, reflected on and discussed the rightness or wrongness of the shooting. The police magistrate at Somerset wrote this in his report: "As the result of the punitive expedition we trust that a moral effect has been produced which the more frequent visits of a man-o-war in these waters will go far towards preventing future outbreaks of violence on small trading vessels."

I spoke to an aged Islander whose father was born on Prince of Wales Island and he remembered a white man's ship which came to Friday Island when he was a boy. He became quite excited when I mentioned the *Sperwer* and said he had heard his "fader talk about that ship." The bags of gold coins taken off the ship before it was burnt became his playthings.

More echoes of the dim past were awakened on Friday Island a few years ago when human skeletons were uncovered at high water mark. A human skull was found in a cave at the top of a hill, and in 1957 a fisherman picked up two sovereigns bearing the youthful head of Queen Victoria. Dated 1867, they were nearly as bright as they must have been when minted.

48

With Christianity established in the Torres Straits, and Thursday Island flourishing as a pearl centre, the pearling industry began to take a hold around Friday Island. A pioneer in the propagating of young pearl shell was James Clark whose work and progress quickly earned him the title of Australia's Pearl King. With such a name he naturally became the target of song and joke for music hall comedians.

He took up residence in Brisbane, his home later becoming the Spastic Children's Home, and appointed a manager on Friday Island to operate the station. Remains of the old jetty, the sturdy landing and housing base for a fleet of luggers, still stand on to remind visitors and inhabitants of busier days around Friday Island.

James Clark also pioneered the Broome waters of Western Australia, where he found rich pearl shell beds and he was the first man to develop diving plant in these waters. In 1917 a Japanese diver operating from one of his luggers found the "Star of the West," the finest pearl ever discovered in Australia. After going on show in a Melbourne jeweller's shop, it was auctioned in London for 20,000 dollars.

Friday Island, at this time, was out-of-bounds to pearlers; it had been taken over by the government as a quarantine station in 1887 and with a leper colony on the south-west end for the following twenty years, Friday Island became inaccessible to all but the authorised.

When the lepers were moved close to Brisbane in 1907 the quarantine station was transferred to Thursday Island. Friday Island, devoid of any inhabitants or activity, took on the aura of a grave-yard.

For an island so lush and picturesque to remain without human contact would have been strange indeed and Mr Norman Hocking, a leading T.I. resident and the manager of the Wanetta Pearling Company, determined to establish the island as an idyllic retreat. With government approval he imported deer from the Dutch East Indies, having once been consul for that area, and Friday Island became the "cradle of deer" in the Torres Strait. It was then officially proclaimed a Flora and Fauna Sanctuary in 1925.

The next memorable event in the tiny island's colourful history occurred on the balmy evening of 29 September 1957, when the luxury troopship *New Australia* collided with the Norwegian oil tanker *Franc Stowe* in the waters near the Island. The troopship was sailing to Malaya, with soldiers and their wives and families aboard, when it happened. Darkness had set in; it was about nine o'clock with both ships near Tuesday Island, and the Torres Strait pilot on duty. To explain the collision there was talk afterwards of "someone not giving the right of way at the right time."

In a dramatic incident, the nose of the *New Australia* jammed into the starboard side of the tanker and each ripped the other open like a sardine tin. Veteran seamen of T.I. were unanimous in their opinion that if the ships had come two inches closer to each other one of them would have sunk.

The 1,000 passengers aboard the *New Australia* were unaware of this danger and no one was hurt. They were not allowed ashore when the ship was taken to lie up at Friday Island for repairs and workers and materials were sent from T.I. for immediate patching-up above the waterline. Tons of cement were used to make a patch for the pierced plates of the troopship. The *Franc Stowe*, less damaged, was able to proceed on her voyage north.

When news of the collision spread, Friday Island was besieged with sightseers from T.I. An enterprising launch owner operated a quick shuttle service at a dollar a head and a press reporter flew from Cairns for a first-hand report. One T.I. resident even received ten dollars for the first picture taken of the damaged troopship. As for the 1,000 passengers, they were said to be most depressed, during the long hours of waiting, by the proximity of the Utopian Isle on which they were not allowed to land.

The Torres Strait pilot was suspended from duty. The *New Australia* is no longer a troopship and is now serving under another name and ownership.

Friday Island, it seemed, was not to lie in peace for too long. A few years after the excitement around its shores, it came to life again. Using Japanese technicians, the Pearl Shell Culture Company transported thousands of tons of baby pearl shell from around the Torres Straits and the cultured pearl shell industry began. An engine room and pump were installed and suitable quarters set up for forty American and Japanese personnel engaged in the venture. Among the buildings that sprang up was one with a plastic roof, the first of its kind in the Straits. Ample fresh water was obtained from a rock well dug thirty-five feet to produce 20,000 gallons a day.

The cultured pearl industry, developed at the famous Mikimoto fishery in Japan, is based on floating rafts which are long, narrow wire baskets, coated with tar and containing ten to twelve selected oyster shells. A tiny piece of shell, like a seed pearl, is carefully placed into each soft oyster of the open shell. This provides the irritant around which it is hoped the pearl will form.

The wire baskets, acting as houses for the oyster shells, are held secure in the water by small concrete blocks which serve to anchor the baskets and protect the shells from currents and water movements. The process had a seventy per cent success rate during its early days at Friday Island.

Family picnics were happy occasions, with boat owners issuing open invitations for a day out-of-doors. Friday Island was a favourite haunt and there was one spot more memorable than others . . . under the largest wild almond tree I saw in the Straits. Many times we rested under its spreading branches and enjoyed delicious picnic meals prepared by the young housewives.

Seawards, huge turtles broke the surface stillness to somersault playfully before diving under with lightning speed. Small children with well-oiled bodies squealed in delight as they imitated a "long tom"; in years to come they would remember the eel-like fish skimming the water like an arrow to escape a larger fish but for the time, they were more taken up with the "catch and go" game and their own inventiveness. Naturally explorative, they loved the late afternoon treasure hunts along the beach and still glistening

51

from their swim they would join the grown-ups in a lazy saunter along the vine-covered foreshores.

For the children there were many forays down to the rocks and much digging into the sand in search of rare coins and relics of early sailing days. Among the finds were pennies minted during the reign of George III and coins dated 1862. The latter, we thought, might well have come from the ill-fated *Sperwer*.

As twilight approached we would clamber into boats and make for home through the molten gold waters that gradually, like the surrounding islands, deepened into the blue of the evening.

8

DIOCESE OF CARPENTARIA

I REMEMBER FROM CHILDHOOD the family album being shown to me and mother pointing out a tall, bearded man in clerical clothes. Mother had said he was Bishop Paterson and that he was killed by black people whom he was trying to help. This incident served only to confuse me at the time; mother's only claim to kinship with this bearded man, who was the first Bishop of Melanesia, being based on the fact that her sister had married into the Paterson family. Later though, when I had learnt more about Bishop John Paterson in the Solomons and the L.M.S. missionary, the Reverend James Chalmers, in New Guinea, I was drawn to the area that had proved fatal for them. Remembering the family connection, I made what could be called a sentimental journey from New Guinea to the Solomons.

The kindly man is widely remembered still with a Bishop Paterson Day held on the anniversary of his death, and the cloth in which his body was wrapped after death is displayed in a glass case in the Honiara Cathedral. In addition, the chalice and Bishop's staff was made from silver plate which belonged to the Paterson family in England.

Inspired by the work of Bishop Paterson and the Reverend Chalmers missionaries flocked to the remote parts of Australia and New Guinea. One man, Bishop Barlow, dreamt of a diocese of Carpentaria as he saw Cooktown, Normanton, and Croydon in north Queensland spring into existence as mining towns. He went to England, collecting thousands of pounds for an endowment fund, and on his return witnessed the formation of the second largest diocese in the world.

In size it was outranked only by Polynesia and for Gilbert White, who became first bishop in 1900 (after having been Archdeacon of Queensland), the area was not only challenging but interesting and beautiful.

Encompassing much uninhabited land, the diocese stretched for thousands of miles to include the Torres Strait islands, Cape York Peninsula, and the northern part of Queensland to within a few miles of Cairns, the Gulf Country, and the Northern Territory. Even Alice Springs in the heart of Australia fitted into the diocese and kept up communications with the headquarters on T.I.

At the time of writing there have been five bishops and each of these has administered to the needs of the mainland Aborigines, the Torres Strait Islanders (after the Church of England took over from the L.M.S. in 1914), and the white Australians. They have lived simply and travelled great distances.

From all accounts the first of them, Bishop White, was a remarkable man. Poet, scholar, artist, writer and orator, he displayed in his work a rich appreciation of communication and the written word. His book *Round About The Torres Straits* is an admirable account of the start and development of missions in the diocese, and another, *Thirty Years In Tropical Australia*, merited the description of "as fine and devoted a work as achieved by any living man."

Bishop White loved to paint in oils and he was the first to put on canvas the eastern coast of the Gulf of Carpentaria. Now his paintings and etchings are of considerable historical value and are housed in the Mitchell Library in Sydney.

The creation of the diocese was an encouraging sign for

Thursday Island is considered a tropical paradise by many southern city dwellers. There is no winter and for nine months of the year temperatures range in the seventies and eighties, with gentle trade winds offsetting humidity. The waters are warm for day or night swimming in shark-proof pools

many Christians and in 1959 the church anniversary of the founding was a jubilant and colourful affair. A procession of clergy, barefooted church wardens, laymen and servers wearing cassocks and white surplices preceded the service in the cathedral. The ceremony was a remembrance of pioneers and martyrs.

Headquarters on T.I. for the diocese occupy five acres of land. They consist of Anglican church buildings, the bishop's house, bungalows for white and coloured priests, and a comfortably furnished house which serves as a "staging camp" and haven for Anglican missionaries seeking medical assistance or rest after illness. The bishop's house has taken on an historical air; it is there that Anglican Church history in the diocese has been determined. It was the scene too of sessions of the first theological college in the diocese. Throughout the grounds are large frangipani trees said to have originated from a cutting planted in the spacious garden of the white-painted Bishopric.

In 1908 Florence Buchanan was ordained first deaconess of the Church of England in north Queensland. For the previous twenty-five years she had been in charge of a daily bible class on T.I. and old residents still talk of her. After ordination she was appointed to the Anglican mission on Moa Island, second largest island in the Torres Strait. For three years she lived alone on the island in a bark hut. A small, frail person, she seemed somehow saintly as she went about her work.

The highest court of the Anglican Church, the synod, meets on Thursday Island every two years. Representatives from all parts of the diocese come together to decide on the business of the church. In 1957 the synod put aside diocese routine for the time and talked through a plan to erect a memorial commemorating the landing on Darnley Island on 9 November 1956 of His Royal Highness, the Duke of Edinburgh.

Prince Philip was the first member of royalty to land on Darnley Island. The imposing memorial was erected on a spot overlooking the sea where Prince Philip had his first swim in the Torres Strait.

TOP: Victoria Parade, running parallel with the waterfront, is the scene of constant pearling activity. Many of the earliest buildings in the township are located on the Parade. BOTTOM: The home of a Thursday Islander. A luxuriant frangipani tree spreads over an outdoor kitchen area

Anglican Sunday School on Thursday Island attracts about 120 children. They gather in the parish hall adjacent to the cathedral or in small groups on the verandah for the lessons given by Islander or white teachers.

At the time of the annual Sunday School picnic these youngsters, along with many others belonging to different churches or attending no Sunday School at all, flock to the wharf for a day out. Aboard mission boats heading for a near-by island they sing happily or talk of the picnic foods.

The organisations, *Comrades of St George* and *Girls' Friendly Society* brought together teenagers in the parish.

Fund raising events on the island were community get-togethers with dancing and turtle suppers. The huge sea turtles, sometimes several feet across in diameter, were cooked in the open. Often the smell of the meat, or the soup cooking, mingled with the salty tang of the air and the almost overwhelming perfume of the tropical flowers.

Being a very active, muscular people, the Islanders were almost fanatical about sport. In basketball they played a tough, fast, competitive game. They met each night on the cathedral courts to play under lights. Spectators cheered wildly for Wongais, Globetrotters, Mercuries, or Wildcats. Lightly and deftly they passed the ball and dodged artfully from one corner of the court to the other. On court the players were almost as exuberant in their ball-handling as were the onlookers bawling out comments and approval.

On Thursday Island many of the church events were interdenominational. Roman Catholic and Church of England fraternities combined for annual fêtes, street stalls, concerts, and sporting activities. One of Thursday Island's worst financial years came in 1959. There was a slump in pearl prices with the development of plastic buttons but still the churches on Thursday Island were supported financially. The Presbyterian fête in that year raised over a thousand pounds, a record amount, and the Roman Catholic Church did not face disaster as it might have elsewhere.

On Sundays rows of Islanders file into the church, filling pews and giving devout attention to the service. In the Anglican cathedral there is no organ but an elderly parishioner, standing in the back pew, plays the drum for hymns which are sung in both English and native language.

At the priest's request for a volunteer to start up a language hymn, there is immediate response. Usually a woman strikes a note, a beat of a drum is heard, and the congregation takes up the song with great gusto. To me the words and music of well known English hymns gain in strength and meaning when sung by the Torres Strait Islanders. "From Greenland's Icy Mountains," "Come Over And Help Us," and "For Those In Peril On The Sea" are among their favourite hymns.

The Islanders sing as if under the hypnosis of an invisible conductor. Triumphant and harmonious notes grow louder, louder, yet controlled, higher and higher, reaching mountainous proportions like waves of the sea, climaxing on the last note of the hymn with perfect timing and completeness.

One overseas visitor, Miss Lilian Schoedler from New York, on a goodwill mission travelling the world in search of unusual people and places, fell in love with Thursday Island and stayed three months. Each Sunday she went to the cathedral and sat enthralled.

Most Torres Strait Islanders have seen no land beyond the strait. They discover foreign places through travellers' tales and films. When people and places of their own environment appeared on the screen, they went wild with excitement. At the sight of skyscraper buildings and crowded streets of capital cities they sat amazed and subdued.

On one occasion there was an electrifying response to a blurred rural scene. A small boy astride his father's knee went into the action of horse and rider. At the same time the audience, almost with binocular vision, picked out the shape of a horse and yelled as one, HORSA! There is no island word for horse but it is an animal in which the Islanders have a great interest.

When Bishop Hudson, tall, distinguished-looking, and with a delightful Oxford accent, returned to his diocese after attending the 1958 Lambeth conference in London he was welcomed back in the parish hall. He told of his visit and doings overseas, the ninety lectures he had given, and conveyed the greetings from overseas branches of the Mothers Union.

His successor on T.I. was Bishop Matthews. Hundreds of Islanders streamed into T.I. on mission ships, luggers, and canoes from Murray, Darnley, Badu, Saibu, Moa, and the smaller islands, for the rare display of war dances in the cathedral grounds. They moved hour after hour to the continual thud of hour glass drums, displaying masculine grace and beauty, vigour, precision, and rhythm to the highest possible degree.

In February 1968, the territory previously served by the diocese of Carpentaria was divided officially and a Bishop of the Northern Territory installed in Darwin.

9

HAMMOND ISLAND

THE TOWN CLINIC ON T.I. was a quiet centre without the emergencies, drastic treatments, and midwifery dramas I had faced in the more adventurous nursing fields of outback Australia or the coast of Labrador.

Sick children were referred to the hospital for comprehensive medical examination. Babies of six months received their preventative anti-tetanus serums and older children their boosters at the outpatients' department of the hospital.

There was no chance on T.I. to advance professionally or enjoy a sophisticated night life. Many young nurses recruited from the south stayed only six to twelve months at the hospital before travelling overseas for professional experience and more adventure.

I felt that away from the technicalities and bustle of modern hospital life I could gain a new concept of nursing. Able to use initiative and imagination I enjoyed the minimum of discipline and found more time to enjoy the local environment.

The atmosphere of the island appealed to me and I read

visitors' books, hunted out newspaper cuttings, talked to old residents, and delved into musty church records dating back to the 1880s.

Weighing babies and advising mothers of another race (when they probably knew best how to care for their healthy children) did not provide excitement but I felt satisfaction in observing, examining, and holding what I thought to be the most appealing babies in the world. They leapt from one stage of development to the next to become sturdy, irresistible toddlers.

Sometimes I was faced with making a decision that did not always turn out to be the right one. I remember well one decision to refer a child to hospital for medical opinion.

A young, unmarried mother came to me with twin girls one of whom, in spite of care and weekly clinic attendance, persistently failed to gain weight. The baby lived with the girl and her mother in a clean home and whenever I visited them, I heard the same story, "Baby good. She smiles, sleeps good. Takes her bottle." It seemed that the child was well but I referred the girl for medical opinion.

An earnest young doctor, unused to handling four-month-old infants, was concerned at her lack of progress. He reprimanded me for not referring her earlier. This was the response, too, of the general nurse in charge of the children's ward at the hospital. The tiny twin was admitted to a cot in the ward, kept under observation for three weeks, fed the same milk formula she had been taking so well before admittance, and discharged without treatment. Doctors could find nothing organically wrong and although it was professionally unethical to say, "I told you so," I did murmur, "Haven't you heard of the frail twin?"

Every day on T.I. was interesting and with cooling breezes off the sea on even the warmest day and with balmy tropical evenings, I was contented.

T.I. lacked the organised sport of cities but we exercised by swimming, day or night, at Hospital Point in the shark-proof pool or playing tennis on the town courts at the other end of the island. We fished off the wharf and went boating at weekends.

When the passenger ship *Waiben* arrived each month from Brisbane social life on the island livened up. The inhabitants of T.I. rushed to the wharf, threw coloured streamers, and joined the guitar playing or singing of "T.I. My Beautiful Home." Visitors, sensing the convivial atmosphere of the island, often stayed longer than intended.

The Italian consul in Sydney, his son, and the author, Ernestine Hill, are among those who have disembarked from the *Waiben* to explore the island. A Melbourne businessman brought his wife and a teenage daughter for a fortnight's fishing, and a young Swedish journalist, loath to leave the island, wrote a series of local features for a Swedish magazine.

During the three days the *Waiben* was in port, round trip passengers to Brisbane bought up pearl shell souvenirs, jewellery, and hand-carved wood. They left their signatures in the visitors' book of the Anglican cathedral, took cruises to near-by islands, picnicked on the sandy beaches they had read about, and swam in the clear blue waters.

At night they watched island dancing. On one occasion only have the Torres Strait dancers performed outside their island home. They went to Brisbane to dance for Queen Elizabeth and Prince Philip. Island craftsmen made a miniature lugger, complete with gold watch chain as anchor, for Prince Charles.

Thursday Islanders fill their nights with laughter, music, singing, and dancing. Hospital nursing aides when off-duty inevitably dance. Flower-decked hair, thudding bare feet, and swinging bodies move rhythmically to the sound of guitars, drums and handclapping. They sang the haunting melodies of their forebears years ago but now many have chosen the mainland pop tunes and use electric guitars for accompaniment.

All Torres Strait Islands have native names but unfortunately they are seldom heard. Kerira is the name for Hammond Island. As clinic sister it was my duty to make fortnightly visits to Hammond and Horn Islands.

Hammond Island is said to have been named by Captain Edwards of the *Pandora* when he was sent out in 1791 to apprehend mutineers of the *Bounty*. It lies three miles out from T.I. and is now an important landmark for ships.

A narrow, timbered island, six miles long with precipitous hills rising to 500 feet, it was considered in the latter part of the last century as a site for headquarters of the pearling shell industry. The government sought a more suitable place than Somerset and a geographical survey reported favourably on Hammond Island as a future place for white settlement.

One of the early explorers wrote: "Hammond Island is a proper place for the English settlement in these waters and the loftiness of the island would doubtless make it a healthy station." It was not chosen by the government of the day as a town site but it has developed in its own way over the years.

Hammond Island had no permanent inhabitants after the second World War but remnants of a past way of life have been found in the hills. Miss McNulty tells of how she and a sister from the T.I. convent had heard that there were "things" to be seen in an old cave at the top of one of the high hills. They followed the directions given them by Islanders and found the large rock cave. Inside was a bundle of human bones tied together with twine, and two skulls, one large, one small, in good condition with perfect sets of teeth. The Royal Geographical Society in T.I., very interested in the discovery, sent a party across to the island to investigate. They found the cave but no bones. Miss McNulty had no explanation for their disappearance.

Hammond Island has had periods of commercial development. A man by the name of Campolly operated a pearling station on Hammond Island seventy years ago; gold was mined in the hills prior to 1914 with good findings being recorded; the Fresh Food and Ice Company, which had refrigerator works on Thursday Island, bred cattle on Hammond to provide meat for the near-by town on T.I.

In 1929 the Roman Catholic Church began a social experiment. Other religious groups had not shown enthusiasm for working on Hammond Island partly because it was so close to Thursday Island and partly because there were so many inhabitants of mixed blood on Hammond, and problems were to be expected.

The Roman Catholic Church took up the challenge and negotiated with the government for use of the land. They founded a settlement on the southern end of the island.

Hammond Island, away from the hustle and bustle of this 20th century, and protected by church and government, earned the name "Island For Children."

Nowadays more than 120 half-castes live at the settlement; more than half this number are under fifteen years of age. Families live comfortably in European-style timber houses. Some of the buildings are on stilts. The houses compare favourably with those of any other settlement in the Straits.

Hammond Island is fringed with coconut palms, wild almond, and paw paw trees. It is forested with tropical growth and contains some of the rarest wild orchids. These are protected in the Torres Strait area.

I first went to Hammond Island on the mission motor launch, the *Little Flower*. It was skippered by the head of a well-known mission family on the island, Francis Durante. He had been aptly described by the superintendent of the mission on Hammond Island as the community's "number one treasure." As an expert, self-taught carpenter, Francis was able to build European-type houses, launches, and dinghies with the skill of a first class craftsman. He could turn his hand to any job that had to be done.

Scattered, red-roofed houses, bright in the morning sun, rose among large green trees to greet the visitor. A Romanesque-style, grey stone building, like the hallowed county church in England, made a striking landmark.

The launch sped past the solid, wartime jetty and Francis skilfully dropped anchor just out from an almond tree sheltering noisy children playing in an upturned boat. I clambered from the launch into a dinghy to reach the shore and had settled into the dinghy, that was bobbing merrily on the water, when another launch sped by. Five green turtles were spread out on that boat. They were bigger than any I had seen previously and I was not surprised to learn that they were on their way to T.I. to be prepared and cooked, Island fashion, for a feast. If they had been sold commercially they would have fetched about five pounds each.

Hammond is a very rocky island but the inhabitants have worked hard to produce gardens: croton bushes, fruit-bearing paw paw trees, sweet potatoes, and runner beans grow around houses; rows of banana trees from a sloping hill top provide food for the settlement. Lime trees, decorative all the year round, grow well but other citrus trees are destroyed by white ants.

Frangipani trees bloom for most of the year. One of these trees near the presbytery bears trailing, wild orchid plants that have been grafted on to lower branches. The orchids range in colour from deepest purple to palest mauve and have yellow centres. They mingle beautifully with the exotic, sweet-smelling, cream and pink frangipani.

The familiar, curly, brown orchid that is found on the mainland grows in wild abandon on Hammond but visitors are forbidden to remove plants from their natural environment. A white orchid found in the bush on Hammond Island was claimed as a rare specimen of good quality and was exported south to be propagated. In that instance the plant did not survive change in locality. Similar attempts to transplant this orchid have failed elsewhere.

Bright purple bougainvillea cascades down the broad. white archway of the convent to shock the senses almost as much as the pervading smell of the frangipani. White-robed Sisters of Our Lady Of The Sacred Heart Order live within the convent and teach.

It is a significant fact that no child of the Torres Strait islands need suffer the insecurity of not being well cared for. The Queensland Government provides a child endowment payment; it is more than adequate to meet the needs of the many scantily dressed coloured children living on remote islands.

The adoption of a child while parents are still alive is a popular and successful practice. One suspects the reason to be endowment payments but the Islanders insist it is

"Island Custom" of long standing. In adoption, it makes no difference if the child is born in or out of wedlock. The Islanders dearly love children and another child is always welcome.

There are many large families on Hammond Island Settlement. One married couple have nineteen children and each one is well cared for and clothed. The eldest son of another large family, Francis Sabatino, is one of the world's best deep sea divers. He trains selected boys to dive and is thorough in his warnings of danger under water. Francis Sabatino was often out for a week or more with his lugger crew in the Darnley Deeps area. This was notoriously known as the Divers' Grave Yard. It was not unusual for him to return after a week with three tons of fine, young pearl shell, valued at one thousand pounds a ton.

Islo Sabatino, a brother, is an expert carpenter who made the model pearling lugger for Prince Charles in 1954. A replica is on show in T.I. in the office of the director of Native Affairs. Lucy, a sister of the two men, is a switchboard attendant at the T.I. hospital.

During the second World War Hammond Island was of strategic importance to the Allies. At Japan's entry into the war the inhabitants of the settlement were evacuated to a suitable place outside Brisbane. The Australian Army took over their island home for four years.

Under military occupation the presbytery building became the orderly room and the convent was used as the officers' mess. Nine-inch guns were pointed out to sea and although the weapons have long been removed the hilltop site is still called Command Hill. Several cement pill boxes lie about the island as reminders of wartime occupation but are too far away to be of any benefit to the Settlement.

Francis Durante was the last civilian to leave Hammond Island when the Japanese made their first air raid in the Straits. He acted as guide to American pilots, based at Horn Island, when the first enemy plane was shot down over Hammond Island. He led them to the wrecked Zero plane; the headless body of the Japanese pilot was found some distance away from the crash.

Children, parents, and teachers returned to Hammond Island in 1946 and have remained there ever since. Since the war there have been other forms of tragedy and heroism. A two-year-old child wandered away from her mother and was found soon afterwards lying face downwards in shallow water. The child's father had left for fishing grounds near New Guinea the day before the tragedy. It was over a week before the news of it reached him.

At 9 p.m. one evening Francis Durante was rowing three women out to the *Little Flower*. Before the dinghy reached the launch that would take them back to T.I., a sudden, big wave rushed over the dinghy and threw them all into the water. One young woman, a teaching nun from the convent, was drowned. Francis rescued the other two and was subsequently awarded the Royal Humane Society Medal for bravery.

The death of a beautiful, eight-year-old girl is clouded in mystery. She was a healthy, robust school child who suddenly developed a sore throat. In spite of prompt attention and early admittance to the T.I. hospital she suffered a worsening of the condition and died of this virulent throat infection thirty-six hours after the onset.

Francis Durante had a South Sea Island mother and a Filipino father. He was slim and athletic and with a skin slightly darker than the light skin of the half-caste. He was born on Darnley Island in the Torres Strait group over forty years ago. He remembers arriving on T.I. at the age of seven, when there were only seven houses, and growing up with a passionate love of boats and fishing.

His close association with the Hammond Island Mission began when he was fourteen. He took on handyman jobs for the staff and revealed a great attention for detail. Settled into his spacious timber house, which he built himself, he lived happily with his devoted wife, of twenty-five years standing and their ten children.

Another of his ambitious undertakings was the handsome, green and tan painted motor launch, the *St Joseph*. He built this from a type of ti tree found in the bush at the rear of the settlement.

66

10

PARADISE FOR CHILDREN

THE BAREFOOTED ISLANDER on Hammond is serene and lighthearted. He appears to be without frustration or restriction and is not in any way adversely affected by the discipline in a Christian mission.

The mission station began over forty years ago but the grey stone church of St Joseph is much newer. It was built in local stone at the suggestion of the priest, Father Dixon. The design chosen was too costly for timber and cement but Hammond Island contained masses of volcanic basalt, one of the hardest rocks known to man. It was certainly available for building purposes but being so hard, it broke many axe-heads and with voluntary labour, the church took two and a half years to build.

When I was on the Island the priest, Father McDermott, said he thought the church should last a thousand years. Some day they would complete the rugged stone interior by lining it with cement and plaster. The building project began soon after the second World War with the purchasing of two Sydney Williams barrack huts from Army disposals. Skilled and unskilled voluntary labour stripped the buildings down and placed the skeleton frameworks at right angles to each other. The resulting shape is a T square. The top "T" measures sixty feet across and twenty feet down. Into the construction went something like 80,000 pieces of heavy stone. Each was carefully moved about until it found a niche and then it was jammed into position by means of stone splinters.

In one day fourteen loads of battleship grey rock were taken out of the hillside by an eight-ton truck; in all, thirteen tons of heavy rock. On the same day the larger stones were cracked and put into the church building. This was no mean achievement for Islanders more used to travelling the seas and diving than building on land.

The church was built without louvres or other standard-type windows that are usually considered necessary for light and ventilation. Seven timber, double doors admit air and sea breezes. Around the high walls, two feet from the trussed ceilings, are cylindrical, concrete tunnels three feet deep. These tunnels are filled with empty, brown beer bottles so that the thick ends of the bottles are inside and the narrow necks outside. The sun, rising in the morning and setting at night, strikes the glass. Shafts of dazzling, amber coloured light, shimmering like dozens of beams from massed spot-lights, ricochet from the rugged, grey walls and the smooth, cement white floor.

On the west end of the building a wooden scaffold construction encloses the huge St Nicholas memorial bell. The bell has a beautiful tone and can be heard daily at T.I. ringing melodiously across the water as it calls the faithful on Hammond Island to prayer.

Night lighting is provided for the Church of St Joseph by means of a thirty-two watt electric generating plant. The sparsely furnished interior is enhanced by carved, wooden altar rails. These and the large, fitted wardrobe for the priest's vestments are the work of Islo Sabatino. A priest visits regularly from T.I. to conduct services and perform sacraments of the Church. Most of the school children are very musical and both boys and girls play the organ in the Church of St Joseph.

On a clear day from the top of the seventy-five feet high hill where the church has been built, the seascape stretches across to Cape York. In the foreground lie Tuesday and Wednesday Islands with the vast expanse of the Coral Sea beyond. The little island of Naghir appears above the horizon to give a mirage effect of being suspended, floating, above the sea. The tip of Cape York rises like a finger pointing to the sky.

To the east of the building lay a white cross which, at the time I was there, marked the only grave in the grassy area of land set aside for a cemetery.

Torres Strait pioneers were buried in the old cemetery facing out to sea at the rear of the settlement. There were about thirty graves and many had imposing, inscribed tombstones and memorial crosses. Some are the graves of young divers who succumbed to the dreaded deep sea paralysis; others of men who helped establish the pearl shell industry at the beginning of the century. A tall, white tombstone bears the inscription:

Pray For Delassa. Beloved wife of Sebascio. Died 17/4/37. Aged 58 years. Erected By Her Sons, Daughters, Grandchildren, And Great Grandchildren.

Mary, the wife of Francis Durante, was a handsome, buxom, intelligent woman with the lighter tan skin of the Polynesians. She reminded me of the star, Bloody Mary, from the *South Pacific* musical. Born in Scotland of a white father and a New Caledonian mother, she supervised distribution of goods from the mission store room and looked after her large family.

Chewing gum was always on hand and given as a reward to children who helped with odd chores. There were no sweets or biscuits on the island and children had exceptionally good teeth. A visiting dentist, commenting on the teeth of Mary's thirteen-year-old daughter, said he had never seen such a perfect set in his long professional career.

The school building of St Joseph's was opened in 1958 by the Minister of Health for Queensland, Dr Noble. It is in an elevated position facing south-east so that it gets the full benefit of prevailing sea breezes. The Australian flag flies from a tall, white pole in front of the school. Double flights of steps and wide verandahs lead into classrooms that are brightly painted. Folding doors, when closed, serve as blackboards. A permanent stage has been built into the structure of the building and a piano provided.

The forty children attending school at the time I was on Hammond Island were taught to grade seven with a Queensland education curriculum. They spoke good English and could read and write well. Both boys and girls learn to play the piano and in singing, can harmonise beautifully in duets, trios and in groups. Handicrafts are encouraged; miniature wooden ships are carved; mats are woven; baskets and exotic fans are made from the dried leaves of the pandanus palm; senior girls and teaching nuns embroider snow-white pillowcases, handkerchiefs, and table mats.

Hammond Island is a port of call for an all-day picnic cruise from T.I. On one occasion a party of *Waiben* tourists found a live dugong placidly lying in the clear waters near the foreshore. According to Miss McNulty, who has spent a lifetime in T.I., the experience is a rare one. She had not seen the sea cow at close quarters.

After a picnic lunch visitors were entertained at a school concert. The children recited poetry, sang native and European songs in duets, trios and groups, and danced in traditional costume and with castanets. Mothers smiled happily at the enthusiastic attention lavished on their chubby, brown-eyed babies in arms. The babies in return gazed with puzzled wonderment at the strangers.

The pleasant climate, the sea, beaches, and bushland made life happy for the children of Hammond Island. They looked forward to swimming, fishing, spearing the occasional dugong, and helping to catch turtles sunning on the reefs. When tired of these activities they dug for turtle eggs in the warm sand. The teaching nuns trained their eager pupils in the competitive games, and at the combined school sports with the T.I. Convent School, Hammond

TOP: A general view of the township on Thursday Island, taken from Milman Hill and looking towards Prince of Wales Island. The population of approximately 2,500 consists mostly of the Islanders, Malayans, and those of mixed blood. About 400 white people are residents engaged in commerce or government activities. BOTTOM: A rainstorm on Thursday Island is a frequent event, since the average annual rainfall amounts to sixty inches. Monsoonal rains alternate with periods of heat and calm for three months of the year

Island children performed with distinction, smoothness, and precision.

On my regular clinic visits to the island from T.I. I was accompanied by Mary Durante. She assembled the lively children, pacified crying toddlers, answered questions, and handled Clinic record cards. The children generally were well-cared for, healthy, robust, and neatly dressed in good quality European cotton clothes. They were comparatively free of ugly tropical sores that disfigured arms and legs of less favoured, coloured children in tropical areas.

Hammond Island is a little known Australian sanctuary. It is an object lesson in providing the simple needs of happy living. It is a paradise for children and is apart from the world of automobile and television. Atomic bombs and other death-dealing missiles have no place on that tropical isle. May it remain as it is. A happy, innocent place.

Top Left: An old resident of Moa Island with glistening white hair against a darkened skin; his eyes squint from decades of strong sunlight. Moa Island is one of the twenty islands of the group. Top Right: Beryl Pilot is one of the cheerful nurses at the Thursday Island General Hospital. Bottom: The dirt roads on Thursday Island are notoriously bad and this truck is obviously a popular form of transportation

11

WRECK OF THE *QUETTA*

THE CIVILISED WORLD of 1890 had not yet been hardened to the loss of lives by the world wars and the sinking of the *Titanic* and *Lusitania*.

The wreck of the *Quetta* on 29 February of that year drew much attention. It went down in the seafaring annals of Queensland as one of the world's tragedies. The wreck occurred on a moonlit night outside Albany Passage near Mount Adolphus Island. The passage is recognised as one of the most hazardous in the world. With the loss of 133 lives, nearly half the ship's complement, thousands of people were stunned by the news of the tragedy.

The *Quetta*, a British India Navigation Company vessel of 3,000 tons, was bound for India from Brisbane when she struck an uncharted rock. The knife-edged pinnacle, running north to south, sank the ship in a few minutes. The Government Resident at Somerset, Frank Jardine, rushed to the scene of the disaster and saved many lives. He sent a mounted, native policeman to the Cape York Telegraph Office, fifteen miles from Somerset, to advise the authorities on Thursday Island of the wreck.

The Queensland Government Survey Ship *Albatross* set out immediately to find the survivors. The rescued crew and passengers were taken to T.I. suffering from exposure and sunburn.

Entries in the *Albatross* made by the skipper, Captain Reid, were:

March 1st 1890. Kept a little steam to go alongside *Quetta* in case she came into port.

2 p.m. *Quetta* loss reported.

2.30 p.m. Raised steam. Took extra stores and medical comforts. Left Thursday Island with Dr Salter, Captain Wilkie (Harbour Master), Rev. McLaren and Mr Ball. Also Ranti, Ferguson and seven volunteers.

5.30 p.m. Got Captain Saunders, Pilot Keating and two Lascars from S.S. *Victoria*.

6 p.m. Took on board 160 Asiatics from Mount Adolphus island. Transhipped *Quetta* people to *Merrie England*.

10 p.m. Anchored for night.

March 2nd 1890. Picked up lady swimming.

A story of courage and endurance lies behind the log book's last entry. "Lady swimming" referred to Emily Lacey, a teenager who stirred Australia by her exploits in the disaster. She spent thirty-six hours in the water. When the *Albatross* reached her she was swimming in shark-infested waters in a state of unconsciousness. She reported afterwards that she had seen people waving from the beach at one stage of her experience, but thinking they were wild blacks, she preferred to go on swimming. Emily Lacey was one of only three female survivors.

The ship's doctor lost his life. The captain was saved from the wreck but it was reported that he never took another ship to sea. Youngest survivor was a little girl who was saved by a Singhalese sailor. Swimming with the unknown infant for over twenty hours, he kept her alive by clasping the body to his chest and putting his tongue into her mouth for her to suck. The real identity of the child was never wholly established. It was thought that she was Mary Copeland, daughter of a widow returning to Scotland with two other children. She was taken to T.I. and adopted by Captain Brown, a Torres Strait Island naval pilot, who had a store in town.

The Singhalese sailor gave up the sea after his experience. He died in the Cloncurry Hospital at seventy years of age, unheralded and unsung for his forgotten bravery.

Appropriately, the child became known as Quetta Brown. When her guardian died a few years after her adoption, she was cared for in Brisbane by his brother and family. She later married the son of this family. Miss McNulty remembered Quetta Brown: "She led a charmed life, that child. Miraculously saved from the *Quetta* wreck, she later fell from the balcony of the hotel and broke her collarbone. Several years after that, she nearly died of typhoid fever. She married and her husband, Captain Brown's nephew, lost his life in the first World War. Quetta remarried and went to live in Southport where she died a few years ago."

Miss Alice Nicklin, whose nephew became premier of Queensland, was the third female saved from the wreck. Frank Jardine rescued the nineteen year old girl after she had been in the water twenty hours.

Divers recovered 200 casks of tallow from the ship's holds. Being in perfect condition they were duly forwarded to England which had been their original destination. The casks arrived almost twenty years after they had been consigned from Brisbane.

A memorial church was built on Thursday Island and consecrated in 1893 as the All Souls Quetta Memorial Church by Bishop Barlow of Queensland. The imposing building stands in spacious grounds of green lawns amid flowering tropical trees and coconut palms. Inside the church near the main entrance is a handsome memorial board that tells in brief the story of the *Quetta* wreck. Above it hangs a tattered Union Jack flag picked up from Murray Island, 100 miles from the scene of the wreck. A lifebuoy bearing S.S. *Quetta* is hanging on the wall.

The *Quetta* over the years was entirely encrusted in coral. Generally, coral grows slowly in Queensland waters and on reflection, one wonders how long it took nature to build the Great Barrier Reef and to make it stretch the 1,000 miles as it does now.

One of the most striking relics in the Memorial Church is a porthole of the ship. The outline and details protrude from beneath the dead coral. It is preserved in glass with a caption that reads, "This porthole was cut from the side of the *Quetta* sixteen years after the vessel was wrecked."

Hanging above the altar in the sanctuary is a light that is never extinguished. It is a symbol of eternal life. The light burns from the old brass riding lamp which once gleamed from the mast head of the *Quetta*. An electric light bulb has replaced the original oil lamp. It shines like a beacon and its pendulum movements seem to swing between pathos and joy.

Other memorials include the font ewer, a copper jug taken from the wrecked *Quetta*.

A stained glass window has been inscribed with, "This tablet is erected with gratitude to Almighty God for restoring one child and also in memory of Kathleen Mary Lacey. Born February 8, 1872. Lost in *Quetta*, 1890."

There is no tower on the memorial church but a wooden scaffold in the grounds houses two bells. The lower one is inscribed: "*Quetta* 1881." Each day at regular intervals its strident notes ring out over the little town of T.I.

Prising the ship's bell loose from the wreck was difficult and the captain of the salvage schooner devised a plan. At low water he tied the bell to the ship's stern and waited for the tide to rise so that when the schooner had been dragged down low, he could cut the rope and release the bell. He was on the point of doing this when the bell came away.

The All Souls Quetta Memorial has been a popular visiting place for tourists. One man to leave his name in the visitors' book was Captain Donaldson, the skipper of the trading vessel *Matunga*. Captain Donaldson was taken prisoner in the Torres Strait during the first World War by the notorious raider *Wolf*. He was taken to Germany and later wrote a book of his capture and life in the hands of the enemy. The book was called *Fifty Years Too Soon*.

Other sea disasters are given space in the memorial church. An inscribed, white marble tablet commemorates the worst disaster incurred by a pearling fleet in the history of Queensland. On 5 March 1899, two hundred miles south of T.I., ships were sheltering down the coast near Cape Melville. Out of a clear sky and without warning of any kind, strong winds ripped down the decks at cyclonic strength. When the cyclone broke, mountainous waves rolled over seventy-three mother-ships and luggers. Of the sixty luggers lost only three were ever raised and three hundred coloured men and three white men lost their lives.

I talked about the disaster with Gordon Vidgen of T.I. whose father was one of the thirty survivors of the cyclone. The day after the Cape Melville disaster, photographs of skeleton vessels lying on the beach near the water's edge had been taken. They were faded reminders of the strength and suddenness of cyclones in the north.

One great story of heroism is associated with that tumultuous time. Mairu Lifu, of Darnley Island, lost her newly-wed husband in that cyclone but she saved the lives of two men by supporting them on her back for several hours. She was a strong swimmer and for this amazing feat of unselfishness and endurance she became the only woman in the Torres Straits to be awarded the Royal Humane Society Medal for bravery. By her example successive generations of Islanders are reminded that the best in human beings, white or coloured, reaches out for others and is capable of stretching out with tremendous courage. Mairu Lifu was highly regarded in her community and when she died, beautiful patterns from powdered coral, shell, and cement were fashioned on her grave,

At Cape Melville a tall, white memorial cross, facing out to sea, is inscribed: "In Memory Of The Pearlers Who Perished In The Terrible Hurricane, March 5 1899."

In the All Souls Quetta Memorial Church on T.I., which later became the Anglican Cathedral of the Diocese of Carpentaria, a marble tablet reads: "When Thou Passeth Through The Waters I Will Be With You." The names of the three white men who perished are listed.

76

Cape Melville had been considered safe; it was viewed as a harbour north of the cyclone belt. The terrible events of 1899 ended the practice of sheltering up there and ever since men have taken their boats into T.I.

The Anglican Cathedral on T.I. is one of the smallest and most interesting cathedrals in the world. It breathes the very spirit of the sea and has ministered to the spiritual welfare of thousands of Torres Strait Islanders, white people, and visitors since the consecration of the All Souls Quetta Memorial Church and the establishment of the cathedral for the Anglican diocese in 1893.

Perhaps the most striking part of the church is the six feet long painted reredos. The white robed figure of Christ rises supreme with outstretched hands as the symbol of Light rising over the Torres Straits. It is a magnificent work superimposed on a light and dark background of sea and islands. In the right hand corner is a kneeling black figure and in the left is a white ship in full sail. The painting is by a southern artist and the kneeling black figure was a local native priest.

A stained glass window in the Douglas Chapel depicts the white-bearded, robed figure of St John of Patmos, with pencil and quill, against a background of sea and islands. The facial features are those of the Honourable John Douglas and in the making of this window a photograph of this much loved man was used.

At the entrance to the chapel is a six feet high rood screen. Albie Inguie, a humble islander, expert carpenter, self-taught craftsman, and devout church member sculptured Christ on the Cross with kneeling angels from wongai wood. Carved dugong, turtle, fish and miniature creatures of the sea embellish the handsome rood screen.

Mrs Annie Dunwoodie, the only midwife in town throughout the early days, is remembered by a stained glass window and a caption that reads: "In Loving Memory Of Mrs Annie Dunwoodie Who Gave Constant and Cheerful Service During Twenty-Six Years of Widowhood In This Town."

The L.M.S. missionary, the Reverend James Chalmers,

often preached in the cathedral. He was the first white man to pioneer the Fly River in New Guinea, was known and loved by Robert Louis Stevenson who lived in the South Seas for some years, and he was the last white missionary to be killed by headhunters. His memorial reads: "To the Glory Of God And In Memory Of The Reverend James Chalmers ('Ta mata'), of the London Missionary Society, Who Together With The Reverend O. T. Tonkins Was Killed By The Natives Of Boarbaha, British New Guinea, On April 1st, 1901, After A Lifetime Of Devoted Service. Presented By His Friends At Thursday Island."

Perhaps above all else in recalling the interior of the cathedral, I remember most clearly the magnificent reredos depicting Christ the King with native priest kneeling in homage, symbolising the coming of the Light to the Torres Straits.

12

BOOBY ISLAND

BOOBY ISLAND LIES on the edge of the Arafura Sea at the north-west end of the Gulf of Carpentaria. It is twenty miles to the west of Thursday Island and thirty miles from the Australian mainland.

As a rock island less than two miles long and with a dome-shaped top scarcely a quarter of a mile across, the island seems at first sight to be uninspiring. Yet it is doubtful if any other ocean landmark has been the scene of such adventure and romance.

Booby Island is a pointer for the great north sea passage which goes through to Bramble Cay and the unmanned lighthouse. Periodic visits are made by the government tender the *Swingle* from T.I., 150 miles away, for the lighthouse to be serviced.

A glistening mica beach attracts sea-faring tourists and the chance to explore a lighthouse area is another drawcard. Booby Island was singled out for a different history from the rest of the islands in the Torres Strait from as far back as 1756. The Dutch ship *Ridjer* sailed in close to the shores and named the rocky outcrop Ridjer's Island.

Captain Cook found this island in the Torres Strait the day after he had landed elsewhere in the Strait on Possession Island and hoisted the flag.

In his diary he wrote: "Mr Banks and I landed upon the island and found it to be mostly a barren rock frequented by birds such as boobies, a few of which we shot, and occasioned by giving it the name Booby Island."

About twenty years later, Captain Bligh and the men turned adrift with him by *Bounty* mutineers sighted the rock from the ship's boat. This entry was made in Captain Bligh's journal: "A small island was seen bearing west. We arrived before dark and found that it was only a rock where boobies resort and for this reason I called it Booby Island."

Boobies are strange birds that resemble gannets. Captain Bligh said of them: "This fish eating bird is as large as a duck. Like a noddy it has received its name from seamen for suffering itself to be caught in the masts and yards of ships. They are the most presumptuous proof of being in the neighbourhood of land than any seafowl we are acquainted with." And then he wrote: "I find that Booby Island was seen by Captain Cook and by a remarkable coincidence of ideas received from him the same name."

Little known and rarely visited, Booby Island is one of the most exciting islands in north Queensland. It has been described as "Rock of Romance," "Haven of Refuge," "Ocean Post Office," and "Treasure Island."

Soon after Cook discovered Booby Island, it became the headquarters for a band of roving Asiatic pirates, probably the only real ones Australia has ever known. With legendary dash and villainy they plundered trading vessels *en route* to the West Indies and the Spanish colony which, at that time, had been established in Manila. It is said that the pirates were finally wiped out by Spanish warships.

Mystery surrounds their rich treasures. Some people believe in buried treasure, and years ago Spanish coins found on the island stirred up new interest in the old legends. One treasure on the island that was found, lost, and found never to be lost again is water. When Booby Island was no more than an ocean landmark, Matthew Flinders discovered a great, hollowed out rock well of fresh water. Somehow the site was unplaced after that. We read later that casks of water were sent from Sydney.

All ships going through the Torres Strait went within view of the rocky outcrop and ever since the first great navigators landed there, it has received mention from explorers, scientists, seamen, and the shipwrecked. They report landing for water. When the casks were empty, they searched for the site Matthew Flinders had marked on his charts, but without success. Captain John Mackay, port master at Brisbane for many years, went to the island years after others had failed to find the well. He surveyed the island with the express purpose of locating the well. He is reported as saying, "Well, that's it! There's definitely no well on *this* island!" and so saying, stepped back and fell down a natural bore in the solid rock. The site was never lost again. Topped with a heavy cement cover, this unique natural tank with a capacity of 7,000 gallons never goes dry.

Another reason for Booby Island to be described as a haven of refuge dates back even farther. When the barren rock was taboo to all Torres Strait Islanders except witch doctors from the Island of Badu, Booby Island was used exclusively for the performance of witch-doctor rites. Other Islanders were not permitted on Booby Island so the rock was safe for shipwrecked sailors and castaways seeking refuge from the sea and headhunting tribes.

With the coming of the white man there were fewer witch-doctors and an end was soon put to their practices but Booby Island remained untouched by inhabitants of other islands. War canoes chasing ships stopped within two miles of the rocky outcrop.

In the early days, ships sometimes struck reefs or were wrecked in the Booby Island area. Captain Bligh, on becoming Governor of New South Wales, and knowing the little rock island, established a food depot for shipwrecked persons. A fifty pound annuity was given and the supply was maintained for many years. The food was stored in a big cave facing the sea. Ships came in on the tide to within a few yards of the cave's entrance. It was a much needed refuge as the nearest port at that time was a thousand miles away. Somerset on Cape York Peninsula had not yet been established as a settlement.

Shipwrecked sailors were not always sure of food in the cave. Usually provisions were replenished by those who had sampled some of the food and been able to plan for others in the same plight; on some occasions though, the cave was raided by mainland Aborigines. Primitive canoes pulled in at the rock and Aborigines took whatever they could find.

In the same cave Australia's second post office was set up. It was started in 1835 by Captain Hodson of H.M.S. *Rattlesnake* and marked as a post office on early charts. The first post office in the colony was the Sydney General Post Office.

In the cave on Booby Island incoming ships picked up mail from the wooden box marked Post Office and left letters and packets to be taken on to England and other parts of the world by the outgoing ships. Those going east and west took mail to Singapore, Japan, and through to London.

Before the post office began, ships on meeting at sea kept up a social custom of recording information about each other for when the ship reached port. This was given to the owners of the ship and to friends.

The Booby Island Post Office became famous while it operated and with the increase in traffic through the Strait, it was not unusual for ships to travel in convoys in case of accident. The founder of the post office, Captain Hodson, began a log book which was to contain information of use to travellers calling in at the island for food and mail. The book was stolen before 1850. The replacement for it was stolen before the turn of the century.

A book, perhaps now long forgotten, entitled *The Diary of a Sea Captain's Wife*, was published in 1830. It records a woman's first impressions of Booby Island. Mention was made of the flagstaff that had been erected by earlier travellers to the area.

Survey ships *Fly* and *Bramble* called at Booby Island on

4 August 1843 and left supplies. And strangely enough they were the first to benefit. Squalls blew up while the ships were surveying the Queensland coast. A ship's boat became separated from the other and work was suspended until a search was made. The boat was not found but much later when a cutter went to Booby Island, written reports of the boat were found in the cave. The missing boat had made straight for the safety of Booby Island. Entries were made in the log book and the crew went on to Port Essington for shelter. The survey ships left further entries and the naturalist of the *Fly* wrote rather facetiously: "Ships *Fly* and *Bramble* hove off to Booby Island for a visit to the Post Office. The log book and some biscuits and a bag of beef were observed. We were rather amused by some of the messages left in the log book, especially by one or two of the fairer creation."

Two years later, boats of an American whaler lost outside the Barrier Reef pulled in at Booby Island. Provisions in the cave saved that crew from starvation.

The Post Office activities continued to increase so that in the 1850s a canvas letter bag marked "Post Master General, Sydney" was added to the cave. At this time the cave held a new strongly bound log book, library books, writing paper, and pen and ink.

The *Sapphire* was another ship to benefit from the provisions. In 1859 she was wrecked on the Sir James Isles inside one of the most used passages through the Strait at that time. The crew took to the boats but the *Sapphire* went down too quickly for any of the stores to be saved. After calling at Booby Island for food the crew went on to Friday Island for water and the men in the captain's boat met death when they were attacked by the savage inhabitants of that island. Stores and provisions were kept in the ocean cave until 1874 but as late as 1920 remains of storage bags were to be found.

A new phase of usefulness was entered into by Booby Island in 1890. A forty-three feet high lighthouse was built of the old rocky outcrop and it stood guard on one of the most isolated areas of the north Queensland coast.

13

I VISIT TREASURE ISLAND

ONLY SINGLE LIGHTHOUSE KEEPERS were allowed on Booby Island before the turn of the century. Each man on arrival was issued with muskets in case of sudden attack by local warriors. Later, families were allowed to be caretakers, and in 1917 the small lighthouse oil lamp was changed to incandescent burners. Nowadays the lighthouse operates a continuous watching coastal station.

Like most others who have heard the tale of Grace Darling, that Scottish heroine of lighthouses, I have always had a yearning to discover more about these remote outposts. I was lucky on T.I. to meet Mrs Jack McInnes whose father, William Norgate, was lighthouse keeper on Booby from 1897 until 1910. Annie Norgat was ten years old when the family went to live on Booby Island. She grew to young womanhood while on the island and went without the benefits of a formal education.

Much later, instruction was available through the Queensland Education Department and at one stage when there were other children resident on the Island, the Queensland government sent a teacher for two years.

The journey across to Booby Island from T.I. takes as long as three hours in a good boat. I made my first trip across on the harbour master's launch which was on a chartered run to deliver stores and mail. It was blowing and raining when I arrived at the wharf but the weather improved as we moved out from T.I. We travelled for miles through the seemingly unending Carpentaria Passage.

My first and lasting impression of that island was that it resembled nothing so much as a huge, grey-brown whale basking on a crinkled sea. Getting closer to the island I could see the tall white lighthouse tower rising defiantly above the surrounding ocean. A row of three white houses with identical frontages gave a look of solidarity to the settlement. Boobies flew over the island. Some rested on the eastern end of the rock but rose and flew off together in a group as the launch dropped anchor. The island rose about fifty feet above the water and when we were almost upon the rocky shore I was able to see the huge caves honeycombing the rock. Some of them were twenty feet across.

Red and brown water marks had been washed around the dome as if the mainland Aboriginal painters had swept in to leave their marks. The lighthouse keeper and his assistant, Jim Best, met us on the water-drenched rock after we had gone ashore in the dinghy. Jim Best, who was to show me around the island, told me I was the first visitor in twelve months.

There are comfortable living conditions for the government employees who stay on the island all year round. The substantial houses, built more than seventy years ago, are well furnished and fitted with an electric light plant of 110 volts. Kerosene is used in stoves and refrigerators. In the yards of the houses I saw storage tanks, cement paths, and rotary clothes lines. A patch of green potatoes and three lime trees struggled to survive in the only area where there is earth . . . a green valley at the rear of the island.

The rock is cut through by caves, passages, and water courses and I was surprised to hear that every known mineral except gold has been found in that rock dome.

Lighthouse keeping has never been without its dangers

and perhaps it is even this that attracts the adventurous to isolated places. In times of illness, help is slow in coming. In the early days signalling with mirrors by day and morse coding at night were the usual forms of communication in times of emergencies. Nowadays, two-way radio is used.

Earlier this century before two-way radio had been established, a two-year-old child of the lighthouse keeper scalded herself. Parents signalled a tanker coming west by Booby Island and quarantine regulations were waived aside in an attempt to get the injured child to T.I. as quickly as possible.

The most common cause for medical attention nowadays is a sting from one of the centipedes that grow to a length of nine inches on Booby Island. Only one small grave lay in the green valley when I was there. It belonged to a child that died at birth.

Jim Best, a tall, lean, likeable Scotsman used to the sea, was an excellent guide. Previously he had been skipper on the mission ship *Reliance* of the Aurukun Presbyterian Mission on the Gulf of Carpentaria.

I was excited at the chance to explore the old ocean post office. A single tree grew out of the rock near the cave's entrance. The seaward opening of the cave stretched through a gloomy passage that was a hundred feet deep and several feet high. Dates and names of a bygone era had been scrawled in jet black rigging paint on the rough surface of the rock walls not far from the entrance. H.M.S. *Salamanda* was clearly decipherable and a date, 1865. *Salamanda* was a great patrol vessel of the last century. Her task was to protect ships sailing the dangerous waters of the Strait.

Jim drew my attention to a date that had been weathered almost to nothingness. It read 1806. In the eerie atmosphere of the unchanged past, I again experienced that strong feeling that being close to history gives. I remembered the moments when I stood in the midst of the evacuated synagogue of Capernaum in Palestine, the ruins of Pompeii, and the ancestral homes of England. It was as if I had come to understand at last the saying, "A thousand ages in Thy sight

A pearling lugger lies at anchor while crew members prepare for further voyages. Each lugger works from a "mother ship," usually a trawler. The best pearl found in Australia in recent years was valued at $4,000 and came from the Torres Strait in 1949

is like an evening gone." Momentarily I reflected on the events of 1806. The journey through the Strait achieved, Matthew Flinders was taken prisoner by the French and left to languish in prison for many years.

One of the latest recorded dates was 1942. In bold black lettering it was a grim reminder that Booby Island was under Army occupation during the second World War. All that remains on the island of Army mess huts used by the men who manned observation, gunnery, and telegraph communication posts are dilapidated sections of corrugated iron buildings. These collapsed like a stack of cards during a cyclone in 1957 and they remain to be cleared away.

There were three children on the island and twelve-year-old Roderick had a life that would be envied by any schoolboy in Australia. He took his lonely environment for granted and was gloriously free from the demands of civilisation, its routine, its mechanisation, and its pettiness. Like many boys of his age he was impatient with regular lessons but he received tuition through the Correspondence School of the Queensland Education Department.

He was a busy boy, fishing all the year round, swimming, collecting shells at low tide, and riding his bicycle along the cement paths between houses. His healthy, outdoor life had made him into a robust child with superb physique and a deeply tanned body. Wherever he went, he wore a brown leather belt over his khaki shorts. This held his most prized possession, a gleaming fisherman's knife.

Perhaps Roderick held the boyish dream of finding elusive pirate treasure on the island. He had explored every cave but at the time I was there, he had found only a few musket balls. Roderick was also something of a bird expert. He knew the names of all the migratory birds that made the island a haven for relaxation and rest. Satin bower birds, brilliantly coloured kingfishers, black moorhens with bright red legs and beaks to match, green pigeons, ducks and geese were among those from New Guinea and the Australian mainland. The warbling blue and yellow honey-eater, with its long beak for picking bees from trunks of trees, comes to Booby Island to die.

TOP: Helmets and air-hose are now standard equipment for pearl divers in Australian waters. In the late 1800s the death rate was extremely high among skin divers before diving dress was first used in the Torres Strait about 1874 by white pearlers. BOTTOM: The waterfront on Thursday Island in the cool of evening. The speedboats at anchor contrast with rowing boats and other slower craft

I spent two hours exploring with Roderick and as we approached the boatshed at the end of my tour, he told me of his pets. There was Timothy the cat, a dog named Lassie, and Thistlehupple, a wild duck. Thistlehupple had been caught on the lighthouse tower. Migratory birds seeking rest on the island do not always land happily. Some collide with the tall lighthouse tower and if caught, freshly dead, they make a tasty meal.

On the boatshed walls hung two gleaming white life buoys that were boldly inscribed "Booby Island." I was quick to persuade Jim to take one down and put it over my head for a souvenir photograph.

Booby Island has not been kind to all visitors. I remember the story of the "Cancer King." In Australia he was a man of questionable character. He left Brisbane on a voyage to the Dutch East Indies in his forty-eight foot launch but foundered on a reef near Booby Island and lost all his possessions. He was saved by a lighthouse keeper who took him to safety but phoned T.I. by radio. Afterwards the "Cancer King" was taken into custody by police. What happened to him after that I was unable to discover.

14

ISLAND WEDDING

AFTER MARRYING, an island couple usually did not take a honeymoon, but a girl married in church liked all the trimmings of wedding finery, gifts, and celebrations.

I remember one wedding where the bride, a tall and graceful Malayan girl, married a white school teacher from Brisbane. The couple had met when he was sent to T.I. for two years by the Queensland Education Department. For their cathedral wedding she wore one of the most beautiful lace and tulle bouffant white wedding gowns that I had ever seen. Her jet black hair was covered with a shoulder-length white veil and she carried a bouquet of cream and pink frangipani. These exotic tropical flowers are free for the picking on T.I. but a posy of the waxen, sweet-smelling flowers in the south would be expensive.

Another coloured girl, reared in a shanty-type home on T.I., married a pearl diver in a late afternoon cathedral wedding. The clothes for that wedding cost two hundred dollars but no one regretted spending on a lavish church wedding.

Once I visited the home of a bride some days before the wedding to see the baby which, like so many island babies, was born out of wedlock. Hanging on a nail in the bedroom her billowy, long white wedding gown looked quite incongruous. It had cost eighty dollars and the bride never expected to use it afterwards. I suggested tentatively that she could hire the frock out for other weddings but this was silently rejected.

With most weddings there are incidents that people remember afterwards, but it is not usual for a traditional bride and her maids to be kept waiting for an hour at the church entrance. On T.I. guests at a wedding on 2 July some years ago remember the bride being left without a man to give her away. The wedding eve had been the anniversary of the Festival of the Light and feasting and dancing had lasted all night.

The bride, a nursing aide from the hospital, wore a long wedding gown of embossed satin, a shoulder-length veil, short white nylon gloves, and sandal-type white shoes that revealed the bare skin of broad, flat feet. The teen-age bridesmaids wore bright pink taffeta frocks that were in perfect contrast to their skins and that set off the white of the bride's gown. A pink net arrangement covered their heads and the wedding trio carried bouquets of artificial white roses. The groom, a widower with two children, had trained at the theological college on Moa Island and had been ordained as a priest in the Church of England. He waited patiently inside.

It was my first island wedding and I went along early to watch the arrival of the bridal party. Islanders are notoriously casual in their observance of time but on this occasion the bride and her maids alighted from a white beribboned taxi a few minutes before 2 p.m. which was the scheduled time for the ceremony to begin. Surrounded by an admiring crowd of guests and onlookers they walked with dignity up the long path to the entrance of the cathedral and waited.

Later I learned that an unusual situation had come about as a result of parental disapproval of the match and that the father had decided at the last minute not to arrive for the ceremony.

A slim, young man, casually dressed, arrived to rescue the bride. He took her left arm and led her into the church, while bridesmaids and guests heaved sighs of relief at seeing the bride's brother.

After the ceremony and signing the register, the couple emerged from the cathedral smiling happily while the rejoicing relatives and friends showered them with confetti and attempted to kiss the bride. When photographs had been taken, a group of islanders gave a display of traditional dancing. They wore lava lavas of all colours of the artist's palette; pillar-box reds, royal purples, vivid greens, indigo blues, each one vertically edged with white lace of various designs and widths to represent the islands from which the men came.

With dark foreheads, ankles, and upper arms decorated with strips of white calico, they presented a fantastic Stone Age contrast to the Space Age. They danced with rhythmic grace and movement to the sound of two short sticks played on an empty petrol drum by a man dressed only in shorts who squatted against a near-by wall. When I inquired as to the significance of this spirited performance from Buzi, the musician, an elderly cathedral bell-ringer replied that it was to make the newly married couple happy. Nothing more, just to make them happy.

After this, the bridal party moved off in a taxi for the customary tour of the island. Later they were entertained by fellow nursing aides at an afternoon tea party in the Nurses' Home.

The real celebrations took place that night in the parish hall when, amid a carefree atmosphere of love, laughter, and island hospitality, hundreds of Islanders swarmed into the reception to celebrate. Chicken broth, tender turtle steak, sop sop, and other native dishes were served to the guests, and this was followed by dessert of tinned fruit and custard.

At that time beer and spirits were forbidden to Torres Strait Islanders but as the evening progressed, toasts were drunk to the health and happiness of the newly married couple in "lolly water" that had been bought locally.

During the festivities I was amused suddenly by seeing a small, sniffing dog steal up behind a shy girl of four or five years. She had forgotten momentarily that she was hiding a piece of turtle meat in the hand at her side. With the dexterity of an accomplished pickpocket, the dog managed to snatch the tempting morsel.

After this reception another display of island dancing was held. In a breathtaking performance the dancers marched in goose step precision to the thud of native drums and the swish-swish of grass skirts. Hand castanets punctuated the sound of the rhythmic, controlled stamping of bare feet. At intervals the dancers retreated into the darkness until the spectators beckoned them back again with lighthearted clapping and singing. It was not unusual for the celebrations to last through the night but I left at midnight strangely subdued by their activities.

15

PRINCE OF WALES ISLAND

PRINCE OF WALES ISLAND, the largest in the Torres Strait group, is one of the most popular tourist spots. It is within easy reach of T.I. and at the nearest point is separated only by a mile of sea. This stretch of water has one of the fastest running currents in the world. The narrow tidal gap is notoriously known as the Rip. When high winds follow the tide during the monsoon season, the Rip runs east and west at fourteen knots an hour. Even modern ships make slow progress here.

Torres Strait Islanders have called this island Muralug or Dead Man's Island. It has a tragic history, is outstandingly picturesque and scenic for the visitor, and provides excellent fishing grounds for the Islanders who go across from T.I.

Hindu coins that were hundreds of years old were found on Prince of Wales Island several years ago. They are now preserved in T.I. in a private museum, demonstrating that the Torres Strait was known to man long before the time of Cook and Flinders. Captain Cook named Prince of Wales Island in 1770. He also named Port Lihou on the same island. The latter took its name from Captain Lihou of the H.M.S. *Zanobia*.

Prince of Wales Island is twelve miles long but has an area of seventy-seven square miles. It is mountainous, the highest hill rising steeply to 750 feet. Along the foreshores a succession of beautiful, tropic beaches sprawl out to provide fishing grounds that teem with fish of good size. Inland lagoons feed duck and other water fowl while crocodiles sleep in fresh water creeks. Birds ranging from sea eagles to tiny blue finches shelter in trees and bushes. Wild deer that had wandered across from Friday Island at low tide, brumbies, cattle, and pigs roam the hills. Oysters cover foreshore rocks, and wild orchids and flowering trees proclaim the area a flora sanctuary.

As lush and sensuous as it is now, Prince of Wales Island had an evil reputation for savagery and violence. Many a tale has been told of shipwrecked crews being killed and eaten by the Muralug natives.

The story that I find most appealing is that of Barbara Thompson and the Muralug tribe. In 1845 Barbara Thompson was the only survivor of the cutter *America* wrecked in the Torres Strait. Thinking that she was the chief's daughter, a spirit child, the Muralug, on finding her, spared her life. She was kept by the warlike islanders for four years and was married to a tribal chief called Boroto. Would-be rescuers from ships did not recognise her when they were within seeing distance, the pale skin had darkened in the hot sun.

Eventually she was rescued in 1849 by the H.M.S. *Rattlesnake* and returned to her parents in Sydney. In 1912 she died at the age of eighty-four. Well-known Australian writer, Ion Idriess, in his book *Isles of Despair* combined fact with fiction to tell the story of the wreck of the *America* and the strange life lived by Barbara Thompson for those four years on Prince of Wales Island.

Far back in the mountains lies a deep, rock pool known as the "dugong". To the Torres Strait Islanders this "dugong" area has grim associations with the past. It was there that the mass shooting of the Muralug took place.

No Torres Strait Islanders will visit that part of the island and the bloody slaughtering has given rise to the oft repeated Dugong Story.

Fifty years ago human skulls were still being found in the area although officially the remains of the Muralug natives were transferred to Hammond Island after the government reprisal. Prince of Wales was deserted for many years after the shooting. It was investigated as a possible site for permanent white settlement but was judged unsuitable due to lack of a harbour for shipping.

No gold or minerals in quantity have ever been found on Prince of Wales but prospectors of another kind are driven to the island. Beneath an overhanging rock at a place called Frenchman's Beach, ancient Aboriginal paintings have withstood time, well protected and undiscovered until several years ago.

The ship *Star of Peace*, beached up on Prince of Wales, brings back memories of an era long past. It served as a coal hulk in the days of sailing ships and what a story it must have of foreign ports. Nowadays it lies up on the the beach, an empty skeleton, but at one time it was the home of a family and each day the children could be seen setting off in their row boat to school in T.I.

A New Zealander by the name of George Joyce is recorded as the first white man to take up land on Prince of Wales Island. He arrived in 1908 and became the island's first permanent settler. George Joyce successfully bred horses for the Java market. They were well-bred, low set, creamy ponies with long manes and tails. He exported fifteen to twenty of these animals each year for an average price of thirty guineas. In the days of sailing ships through the Strait, transporting these animals was a dangerous enterprise but the trading went on until the outbreak of war in 1914.

Soon afterwards, George Joyce died but the property was taken over by his son, Frank. For more than fifty years this well-built, powerful man, has been one of the most popular and best known identities in the Straits. Frank Joyce revived the export trade of horses commenced by his father. He bred racehorses for southern markets and bought up a blood stallion from the famous Valley of Lagoons Station in Brisbane. A new export trade with the Dutch East Indies was started up as well.

Before the second World War Frank Joyce decided to breed cattle on the island. Previous attempts by others had failed but during the war he made history as a successful cattle man and as cattle drover under contract to the Army. Old-timers still talk of the time he drove thousands of bullocks from down south to Cape York. After that thousand mile trek he took the animals, in relay, by punt across to the Prince of Wales Island for slaughtering.

Yards had been erected for the killing and meat supplies went out for thousands of Allied troops. Frank Joyce worked with cattle for the Army from 1941 to 1946. Long, hot, dry seasons in those eventful years made feeding very difficult for him, and crocodiles in inland rivers snatched many of the young stock. When the war ended, Frank Joyce settled back to breeding his own cattle. He introduced Poll Angus breeds to increase the strain and met the meat demands of the civilian population in T.I.

For nearly fifty years he pulled his dinghy across the narrow tidal rip and survived mishaps. He had been known to prophesy that the rip would get him in the end but when his boat overturned, the shock must have been too much for him. He was rescued immediately by his companion, an Aboriginal boy from Aurukun Mission in the Gulf Country, but could not be brought back to life.

For his brave deed the Aboriginal boy was awarded the Royal Humane Society's silver medal.

Frank Joyce's widow moved to T.I. and leased out the cottage built by her husband. Near to "Joyce's Cottage", as it became known, are the remains of an old stone jetty built by two of the early settlers. When the Maoris, Johnny and Billy, moved away the site took on the quaint name of "Johnny Maoris".

Most maps of Torres Strait do not mark Port Lihou but it is an idyllic spot, rather like a little bay. More than any other part of the Torres Strait landscape, it fulfilled my dream of what a Robinson Crusoe island should be like. Water streamed from rocks; wild berries grew in trees; shoals of fish sped through the clear waters. A quarter of a mile inland from the beach a permanent rock pool entices those in need of a cool drink just as it did the early sailors seeking water supplies. Rows of coconut palms growing from forty to sixty feet high line the foreshores and spread their green fronds out across the sands.

For the visitor the most striking part of this bay is the towering rock formation a few yards up from the water's edge. A huge wall of rock boulders reaches skywards and the rocks nestle precariously against each other. This formation was first recorded by Matthew Flinders. The brown colour of water-washed rocks has in this instance given way to a new covering. A thick coating of verdigris had me proclaiming on first encounter that a layer of sulphur powder lent new colouring to the boulders.

The bush is heavily timbered with blackwood trees which, at one time, might have been felled by a southern company for sawmilling. Nowadays, most of the timber is cut into four feet lengths, taken to T.I. in barges, and sold for fuel.

On the opposite side of the island to Port Lihou, picturesque Sunrise River beckons fishermen with red and white schnapper, barramundi, and black trevally. Lying a short walk away is a swamp, the home of the berdigan and the spoonbill duck.

Port Lihou proper is one and a half miles long. It once gave shelter to the 5,000 ton German raider, *Wolf*, which laid up for careening during the first World War.

Many of the stories I heard of the Torres Straits came from Charles Garvey. A veteran coxswain of the T.I. harbour master's launch, he had spent thirty-five years with the Queensland Harbours and Marine Department with most of his time in the Torres Straits.

Wolf was fitted with 5.9 guns and carried a small seaplane. Her top masts and funnels could be lowered at any time and she was one of the most feared and most successful enemy ships. When *Wolf* went safely back into

German waters she took with her hundreds of prisoners and much valuable cargo.

The Burns Philp trading vessel *Matunga* was one of her victims. The skipper, Captain Donaldson, was on his way from Sydney to New Guinea with a load of coal. The Germans intercepted a wireless message and the *Wolf* caught up with her the day she was due into Rabaul. A German officer went aboard and in perfect English courteously addressed Captain Donaldson, "Good Morning, Captain Donaldson. We expected you two days ago." I was reminded of an historical meeting in the heart of Africa when the immortal words, "Dr Livingstone, I presume" were courteously addressed to the great explorer by his friend Dr Stanley. Captain Donaldson, his crew, and passengers, were taken prisoner by *Wolf*; the *Matunga* was sunk by bombs on the other side of Dutch New Guinea.

In November of 1917, wireless parts and other equipment were washed up on the beach at Halmshire in north-west New Guinea. They were found by a T.I. resident who identified pieces as belonging to the *Matunga*.

In recent years a South Sea Island family has leased four acres of land at Port Lihou to grow vegetables. The rich black soil grows bananas, paw paws, sweet potatoes, water melon, pumpkin, and tomatoes to perfection.

Temporary shelters for weekend or holiday occupation have been built by the Bourne family. Michael Bourne, middle-aged head of the family, is following on after his father who was the first Samoan to work land at Port Lihou. The son made many plans for his farm and hoped to lay pipes from the natural spring.

When not working on the T.I. wharf, Michael Bourne took his wife, several children, and relatives to Port Lihou to help cultivate the land. They lived in two old, corrugated iron huts, roughly assembled, and blotting the landscape in their ugliness. Close by, an entirely different structure had been put up for outdoor living. Made of coconut palm fronds, it reminded me of a rustic bough shed in the inland of Australia where the walls and roof let in the coolness of outside breezes. The women plaited strips of palm leaf so that they could be placed upright in some places to send the rain running off the surface. The bush timber uprights came from the mangrove swamps and were as straight as poles. Some had been sixty feet high with no branches and only a few leaves at the top. They were wonderful posts for tall, big buildings, so straight, and no joining required.

Michael and his family tried in a small, commercial way to profit commercially from the coconuts growing around Port Lihou. Coconut oil was made on the spot but the method was slow and primitive. A simple implement was used in the first long process of grating the white flesh of the nut. The flesh was then squeezed in a thin, cotton material resembling muslin, and the resulting white fluid left to stand for some hours. In the final stage, a clear oil rose to the surface of this milky substance. I was surprised to learn that as many as ten to twelve coconuts were required to fill one lemonade bottle.

Coconut oil is used in cooking and among Island people it is applied to the body from the first week after birth, to keep the skin smooth, shining, and protected. It serves, too, as an effective laxative.

A real danger in a living area surrounded by coconut palms are the falling nuts. Children have been killed by the force of a blow on the head from a ripened nut.

I remember that when I was at Port Lihou, I was extremely touched by the tenderness of the children. In the forked branch of a small coconut palm rested half a coconut shell that was filled with a white, moving ball of fluff. It was a rare Torres Strait pigeon, about two weeks old, which the children had found in a mangrove swamp. They kept it alive with pellets of damper and coconut milk.

Once these nutmeg pigeons, famous migratory birds, flew overhead in hundreds and thousands during the summer months but they were killed off during the breeding season, first by the Islanders who wanted the thick white plumage, and next, by the white man on his arrival in the Straits. It is unusual now to see more than ten or fifteen of these birds together, and a visitor is fortunate to see one nutmeg pigeon.

Another popular place on Prince of Wales Island for picnics and fishing excursions is Bamfield Heads. Fairy-like, pale green casuarinas growing from the smooth, white sand close to the water's edge, form a fringe to this secluded beach.

Masses of brown rounded rocks, gently washed with water, are completely covered with oyster shells. These are known locally as milk oysters and cement themselves in crowded communities on the hard surface. Their shells are not the familiar dark grey colour but off-white and blending to light grey at the scalloped edges.

All that anyone needs for a feast of oysters is a small chisel or pick for dislodging the outer shells from the rocks and then a blade or knife for opening shells. The oysters on the rocks are washed continuously by the sea water and the salty tang of them when they are broken open is unforgettable.

Although wild life was plentiful on the island and birds scattered in the trees at the sound of approaching strangers, native wallabies were not to be found. They were plentiful on Friday Island but did not swim the stretch of water separating the land masses. A rough bush track, two miles long, led visitors along the shaded, rocky, dry river bed, and then up a rugged cliff face, to the deep rock pool. Ribbon-like dark bands had been made on the towering grey cliffs by thundering waterfalls of the monsoon season.

With obsessional interest in the past and the rituals of the tribes in the pre-Christian era in the Straits, I thought of Barbara Thompson and visualised her in the mountain pool with slim, naked body unused to the tropical sun and and ravaged by sunburn.

A slim, blonde English nursing sister in her twenties seemed the prototype of Barbara Thompson. She loved picnicking at Bamfield Heads and is probably the only trainee of the famous St Thomas Hospital, overlooking the Thames at Westminster Bridge, to come to the top of Australia on a working holiday.

She nursed at T.I. Hospital for six months and returned to England to take up a staff appointment at the august institution where Florence Nightingale founded the first nursing school. She stood on the foreshore rocks in swimming costume and gazed wistfully out to sea; an English rose who gave the impression of a water nymph thoroughly at home, revelling in the freedom of a unique, new environment never likely to be forgotten in years ahead.

Prince of Wales Island offers every inducement for development but until recognition comes to it, the beaches, spring water, mosquito-free nights, and an ideal climate for nine months of the year will continue to attract the last remaining pioneers, week-enders, and holiday-makers.

Separated from Prince of Wales Island by a sea passage one hundred yards wide, tiny Packe Island lies west of Port Lihou and is seldom visited by ships. A lone Greek lived there for years and kept his sanity by working on scientific experiments with the oyster. He found some success in pearl culture before modern methods were developed.

His successor was an energetic, red-headed Swede, aged thirty-five. He was content in his solitary existence, welcoming the occasional visitor, drying fish, gardening. He had built himself a comfortable shack, a drying rack for fish, dug a seven feet deep rock well for fresh water, and surfaced earth paths with crushed oyster shells. His diet consisted mainly of fresh fish, bananas, paw paw, and vegetables from his garden. At that time he wished for no other life.

16

CHILDREN'S CONCERT EXTRAORDINARY

WHEN HORN ISLAND Settlement children packed audiences into the T.I. Town Hall for their concerts on two evenings, Willie Namie stood as master-mind at the back of their success.

It was the first time a public performance had been arranged, produced, directed and staged by a Torres Strait Islander. He attributed his success to experience gained on Palm Island Aboriginal Settlement where he was part of the local concert group. The concerts raised about one hundred and forty dollars for St Paul's Anglican Mission on Moa Island which ministered to the Horn Islanders through a native-trained priest, Father Banu.

The T.I. Town Hall is a well built, spacious wooden building with broad open sides admitting fresh air, stage, piano, and a good timbered floor that can be used as a ballroom. It was in the care of the town clerk. A mammoth canvas stage curtain, measuring sixty feet by twelve feet, hid the scurryings between items and gave the audience a realistic painting of the local harbour and waterfront as seen from the top of Milman Hill, highest point on T.I.

TOP: Prawns are a major export from the Torres Strait since the introduction of trawlers in the post-war years. The industry has helped the island economy, especially during the decline of the pearl shell when plastic buttons were introduced. BOTTOM: A peaceful view from Milman Hill, Thursday Island, looking towards Prince of Wales Island, the largest in the group. Separated by only one mile, the latter island is one of the most popular tourist spots

The canvas had been painted by a young school teacher posted to T.I. by the Queensland Education Department.

A middle-aged Islander, appointed at the last moment to replace another, was Master of Ceremonies. He made an incongruous figure, dressed in gay American-style cotton shirt over khaki cotton trousers, and woolly head decorated with red hibiscus flower and colourful leis around his neck. He was as unsuitable for the task of introducing items as Fred Astaire would have been in the role of Henry VIII. When he swaggered on to the stage the audience lost the name of the item in laughter.

By contrast, the producer was an unobtrusive man who came on stage for the group singing of the National Anthem and did not appear for the rest of the evening. Willie Namie replaced his traditional island dress with dark blue trousers, a long-sleeved white shirt, dark bow tie, and bare feet protected by sandals for the evening.

The first half of the concert resembled that of any school concert on the mainland. There were English and Australian ballads and songs, and such melodies as "Galway Bay," "Powder Your Nose with Sunshine," and "Sundowner" sung to the tune of "Danny Boy." The Island children excelled in singing English hymns and Negro spirituals unaccompanied. Dressed neatly in European clothes they were as scrubbed as any suburban children in Australia, boys immaculate in white shirts and red bow ties, girls prim in their pleated skirts and blouses.

In my experience the Horn Island children were astonishingly shy when spoken to by Europeans, but on stage they were jubilant and confident. One child gave an object lesson on the humble trochus shell:

The trochus shell is a sea shell. The shell of the trochus is shaped like a pyramid or cone. It is a white shell with pink stripes. The snail inside is removed by boiling the shell. The trochus is found on the Great Barrier Reef and smaller reefs of the Strait. No shell measuring less than two and a half inches is allowed to be picked. The trochus is useful in making buttons and collar studs.

TOP: Thursday Island has two prominent features, Milman Hill and Green Hill. This view of portion of the township was taken from Green Hill, with Prince of Wales Island in the background. BOTTOM: A view of sideshows at the Bamaga Annual Rodeo and Agricultural Show. Bamaga is a native settlement of Torres Strait Islanders, originally from Saibu Island near the New Guinea coast. It is the most northerly community on the Australian mainland, fifteen miles south of Cape York.

Before the war, Japan bought Australian trochus but now it is exported to the United States of America.

At the mention of the United States, Islanders clapped and cheered. I took it to be a gesture of appreciation for what the country was doing in time of the greatest slump in the Torres Strait pearling industry.

A picturesque mime called "Boarding the lugger and spearing the Dugong" depicted familiar scenes of Torres Strait living. Eight small boys, immaculately dressed in blue shorts, white singlets, and jaunty sailor caps, translated the unspoken word into decisive actions with imaginative vigour. They acted out boarding the lugger, spearing the dugong, and finally, with confidence and facility, they demonstrated the final thrust by long-handled spears to end the life of the captured seacow. The performance was a masterpiece of co-ordination, with precise action and imaginative body movements bringing loud applause and an encore for the young participants.

For the second half of the concert the entertainment leant towards the traditional. Horn Island children, whose forebears were among the most savage in the Torres Strait, swayed, danced, and chanted to the compelling strains of steel guitars, castanets made by them, and the resounding thud of short sticks on empty petrol drums. The earnestness of the young players conveyed an impression of traditional worship rather than showy display and in the interpretation of ancient tradition the past was made meaningful even to the very young onlookers.

In one item two rows of small boys seated themselves cross-legged at the front of the stage facing each other. One row of boys strummed guitars and the other kept time with shakers held aloft. The ingenious rattle was made from empty coconut shells filled with hard seeds of the wongai tree nut. The outside of the musical instrument had been made smooth and been painted a bright colour for dances, festivals, and ceremonials.

To the music of these boys, hip-swaying, hand-twisting girls aged between ten and thirteen years, edged their way on to the stage. By European standards they looked much older, resembling dusky-skinned Polynesian dancers rather than school children. Arms, ankles, hair, and neck were decorated, Island fashion, with rosette circlets of red and white crepe paper. The background thud of swift-moving drum sticks gained frenzied momentum as the barefooted dancers moved in unison to the centre of the stage. With fluid movements exaggerated by their tight-fitting skirts, they moved with graceful control and a sustained sense of rhythm. Hands moved in accord with the body and the youngsters danced as if mesmerised.

In another item, the older boys performed an ancient dance of their forebears. They gave a spirited, interpretative display, called "Breaking the Waves," that was familiar to generations of Islanders. Ten boys, dressed in grass skirts fashioned from narrow strips of coconut palm fronds over brilliant red lava lavas, wore spectacular, hand-carved mitre head-dresses as used by warriors of old. The head-dresses formed a carved arch around the face as they stretched from forehead to lower jaw line. Eye-arresting fans projected from the back of hands. They were made from light timbered frames covered with snow white feathers plucked mainly from the Ibis. As the hands moved with lightning speed the fans flowed and waved to produce the cumulative effect of white sea foam, giving credence to the title, "Breaking the Waves." Lightly stamping bare feet, flexing brown knees, swishing grass skirts, the girls twisted, turned, and swayed with lightning speed as they moved in unison to the accelerating guitar music and the realistic rhythm of swaying white feathers.

Senior girls performed a dance called "Queen of the Dance." A buxom fourteen-year-old girl took the star role and the youthful dancers wore grass skirts over gay patterned briefs and matching bras. Colourful leis of red and white crepe paper adorned the dancers and each girl carried a pair of clickers in each hand. The clickers were cut from dried bamboo, three or four inches in circumference, to a length of eighteen inches, and were then split down the centre for about five inches. They were painted red and had white stripes and island motifs super-imposed. When vigorously shaken in unison to the rhythmic movements of the dancers, the distinctive loud clapping sound of the clickers seemed the perfect medium for synchronising. The moulded brown limbs of the girls in "Queen of the Dance" leant out provocatively beneath grass skirts as the lithe dancers moved about the stage.

The climax came as they gracefully formed into a semi-circle, chanting as if hypnotised, and clacking their hand instruments with almost frenzied movements. To this animated scene the resplendent Queen danced slowly. She wore the same regalia as her subjects but had added a spectacular crown made from gleaming aluminium paper foil and red crepe paper. The weird chanting and clacking sounds continued unabated as dancers came forward, one by one, to greet the Queen and kneel in homage.

The grand finale to the concert was the farewell hula dance, a sparkling song and dance number in which boys and girls combined to bid the audience a boisterous and happy farewell. There were no floral bouquets thrown on stage at the final performance, no curtain calls for the man behind it all, and no free supper for the performers.

It was nearly midnight when the party left for home with personal belongings packed in suitcases and cartons. Some of the youngsters would rise at the customary hour of four o'clock in the morning to fish for their breakfast off the Horn Island jetty.

17

GOODE ISLAND

GOODE, A SMALL ISLAND four miles out from T.I., is one
and a half miles wide, with great boulders and rocks along
the foreshore contributing to the rugged landscape. Inland
the surface is very rocky but trees grow almost miraculously
among the rocks. The highest hill rises four hundred feet
above sea level and although Goode Island is practically
uninhabited nowadays, it was well known to hundreds of
Australian soldiers during the second World War.

Migratory birds of many species including the bee-eaters,
dollar birds, oriolas, and satin birds, rest up in the trees
during their annual procession.

In the *Investigator* in 1802 Matthew Flinders dropped
anchor on the west side of the island and with botanists in
the party landed on the rocky site to take bearings. He
wrote in his diary, "The stone is granite and porphyry.
In one place I found streaks of verdigris as if the cliffs above
contained copper ore." Matthew Flinders named the place,
Goode Island, after the gardener with the expedition,
Peter Goode.

At one time Goode Island was a coaling station for the

refuelling of passing vessels and warships that guarded the Torres Strait. Offshore an old iron hulk reminds visitors of the leisurely days of sailing ships when old ships served as coal hulks. The *William Fairbairn* is said to have been the fastest tea clipper on the run to the East.

Goode Island was established as a pearling station with a fleet of luggers, a boat slipway for repair of vessels, spacious buildings like the manager's residence which boasted a billiard table, carpenter and blacksmith shops, and there was a house on top of the hill for the Lloyds of London representative. A manned lighthouse was established in 1882 by the Commonwealth Lighthouse Service. It continues to operate and provide for the safety of men and ships.

Harrison Buoy, two miles out from T.I., is the northern terminus of the Torres Strait Islands Pilot Service. This organisation navigates vessels along the treacherous north Queensland coast down south to Sydney. More than 1,000 miles long, this is one of the worst sea passages in the world.

Before the expansion of the service in 1884, Goode Island accommodated a resident harbour pilot who guided south and north bound ships into Thursday Island harbour. A T.I. pilot identity, Captain Gerald Bruce, recalls the days when his father, a master mariner, was harbour pilot and used to travel in a ship's long boat with a crew of eight.

Nowadays, thirty licensed pilots have been provided with housing on T.I. and work from the Island on a roster system. Each of them spends six days at sea and when working the hazardous passage north of Cooktown on the Queensland coast, scarcely a night is spent in bed.

A pilot usually travels by air from Horn Island to Brisbane or Sydney to board the northern bound vessel. After piloting the ship through the reefs he returns to T.I. by motor launch or boards a southern bound ship.

The port master at Brisbane, John Forrester, years ago introduced the fast, comfortable launch used today by the Queensland Coast Pilot Service. The spotlessly clean, white painted launch lies at anchor in the T.I. harbour and a bright red flag waves from the masthead when the pilot is aboard.

Most Torres Strait pilots are robust, middle-aged men, agile enough to clamber up thirty or forty steps of a rope ladder dangling from the ship's side. Once the pilot puts his foot on the first broad tread of the swaying ladder and begins to ascend, the engines increase revving and the motor launch and crew return to T.I.

During the first World War, a small Australian Naval Station was based on Goode Island for the signalling of ships at sea. During the second World War, Army personnel were in full occupation, and medical services included a general hospital. Nowadays, water tanks, rusted barbed-wire entanglements, petrol drums, an underground munitions dump, and concrete foundations lay strewn abroad like the ruins of a modern city.

Goode Island lighthouse was converted to automatic during the second World War and a transmitting and receiving radio set installed to operate as a one man, day-time radio signal station. From the highest point on the Island, the lofty white tower rises over 400 feet above sea level. It is a fitting memorial to the period when the Torres Strait was a much used highway to the East.

Mrs Jack McInnes, of T.I., lived on the Island when her father was lighthouse keeper from 1897 to 1910, and she remembers that at that time there were several children attending school.

The officer in charge of the Goode Island lighthouse logs weather findings, investigates navigation possibilities, contacts passing ships by morse code, uses a two way Hellecraft radio set from Germany with a hearing range of sixty miles, and has a portable radio set to receive programmes from Radio Australia, America, Japan, and New Guinea.

An important landmark near Hammond Island, Hammond Rock, has sharp contours and a red light that serves as a warning of submerged reefs in the area. A Japanese ship, the *Tanga Maru*, went aground on a reef in this area some years ago. The ship was travelling north loaded with bales of Australian wool. In an attempt to refloat the stricken vessel, the valuable cargo was unloaded from the holds, transferred to the *Kallatina*, which belonged to the John Burke Shipping Company, and taken to T.I. The *Kallatina* made two trips a day from T.I. to the *Tanga Maru* to unload the wool and from T.I. wharf, trucks took the bales out to the recreation grounds and other open spaces for unloading.

A bare, deepwater rock, called Black Rock, gives the sign of safe anchorage to overseas vessels and was also a favourite fishing spot for experienced T.I. fishermen.

Lighthouse keeping offered more a way of life than a job, and when I visited Jack and Molly Crawford and their three children on Goode Island, I was not surprised by their happy existence. They had left Scotland for the tropical climate of north Queensland and had spent two years at the Sandy Bay lighthouse on Fraser Island, about three hundred miles north from Brisbane, before travelling much farther up the coast to Booby Island and then settling at Goode Island. Their visitors were mainly men from passing ships; occasionally friends from T.I. called in at the lighthouse. Molly Crawford, charming and dainty, expressed no longing for adult female company and she happily filled her days with chores about the lighthouse and cooking and sewing.

The gale force winds of the bleak Labrador coast, the hot exhausting breath of the Australian Inland, the penetrating winds of the Palestinian winter could not compare in velocity, intensity, persistence or perpetual sound with the strong hurricane winds that swept and howled around the summit of Goode Island for nine months of the year. Yet with the casualness of thought and word with which one might comment on the temperature of daily weather, Mrs Crawford simply remarked in her broad Scottish accent, "Sometimes the wind gets on our nerves. Usually we do not even notice it."

In some areas of the station nothing will grow because of the fierce winds. Tomatoes grow surprisingly well in season in protected corners, and with apples and pawpaws provide welcome additions of fresh fruit to the daily diet. A small

110

lemon tree grows on the lee side of the island and gives hundreds of lemons every year.

The children's pets, Bullie, a plump female dog of mixed pedigree, and Pedro, a corello, along with sixteen laying hens and three white turkeys, made up the island menagerie. To the Crawford family, Bullie was a real lighthouse dog. She could tell when a launch was moving towards the lighthouse even before it came into sight and would bark loudly. The cute-faced corello showed complete contempt for strangers and was chained by one leg to a croton bush.

The government light tender, the *Swingle*, took stores and mail to Goode Island and Booby Island twice a month. On arrival at Goode Island the stores were hauled up the steep concrete track in a small trolley operated by a cable.

A six-hundred-ton light tender based at Brisbane, the *Cape Leewin*, makes regular trips along the deep waters of the Queensland coast to repaint floating buoys, replace lighthouse gas cylinders, and check automatic lights on inaccessible islands and reefs. When required, the ship takes heavy equipment to Goode Island by army duck.

I had long looked forward to seeing over the lighthouse and Jack Crawford was a friendly and communicative guide. He explained the marvellous working of a robot coastal watcher and how all the important lights are precision instruments accurate to a fraction of an inch, with a reliability proved in many years of uninterrupted service.

On the tour of inspection, my chief delight was climbing the narrow, winding tower stairs to stand on a small platform near the top. Through the lighthouse telescope, I gazed out over the sea and all the landmarks whose history so fascinated me.

In a narrow circular area lower down the tower the automatic sun valve, protected by an oval-shaped glass dome two and a half feet high, was a breath-taking sight. It radiated glorious colours in much the same way that a rainbow is formed by sunshine passing through raindrops. The contour of the lens with built-up sections to act as prisms resembled rich, iridescent glass crystal. A glass cylinder, containing a metal tube coated with carbon-

111

dioxide, is placed in a position exposed to a pilot light. Although this expands the tube only a fraction, it is enough to depress a small spring regulating the gas supply and cut it off. At sunset the tube contracts, allowing the lever to rest a fraction of an inch, opens the nozzle of the gas tube and refuels the light which burns and flashes white until sunlight again reverses the process.

In a small office where nautical wall maps and detailed charts had been hung, I listened to the regular midday wireless communication schedule from Booby Island. The dramatic opening of the Goode Island call signal, "W.J. 4 B.L. calling Booby Island V.L. 4 B.A." caused me to think back on the vastly different atmosphere of Innamincka in Central Australia. There communication by morse code and pedal radio was carried on over a distance of six hundred miles.

I learned as well that it was unknown for an automatic beacon to fail but in the event of it happening, a battery-controlled light could be substituted.

Goode Island was an exciting place for me but at Christmas time the T.I. shops were obvious places to enchant the children. Little Gaye had never been to a party and the promise of the annual community Christmas party on T.I. with the traditional Santa Claus distributing gifts from a glistening tree, a puppet show, and a magician had her on edge with excitement for weeks before the event. I knew the feelings of the children and several days before the party when I received a letter from one of them, I was moved almost to tears. It read:

Dear Sister,

Thank you for inviting me to the party but I will not be there. Daddy will be alone and I would rather stay with him. Mummy, Ron, and Gaye will tell me all about the party.

Yours truly,
Ian.

Lighthouse keeping on Goode Island was a happy and binding life for a family.

18

TROPICAL PARADISE

ONE AND A HALF MILES from Goode Island lighthouse station, a rugged bush track leads downhill to a red-roofed holiday home that nestles among green trees near a palm-clad shore. Mr Norman Hocking and his charming wife, leading T.I. residents and members of two of Brisbane's oldest families, have established a charming home and provided a refuge for southern friends seeking to escape the colder winters.

Norman Hocking's uncle founded the present Wanetta Pearling Company in the nineties and, for a short time, was in partnership with James Clark, Queensland's Pearl King. Mrs Hocking, a prototype of Queen Mary, was a handsome southern woman who kept up her elegance and social charm while rearing a family on the small island.

Visitors to this island home were frequent. Among those who relaxed in the cane lounges and easy chairs of the verandah was Lord Kitchener who had gone ashore at Goode Island to inspect for defence purposes before the first World War.

Retired Australian Army leader of the first World War,

Major General Julius Bruche, for many years avoided southern winters and made Goode Island a favourite annual resort as guest of the Hockings.

Lady Bisset, wife of the commander of the *Queen Mary*, Lord Stonehaven, who was Governor of Australia at one time, the Dutch Consul for Queensland, Mr Teppama, and former High Commissioner for Australia in London, Sir John White, and Lady White, visited as well. A more recent visitor to Goode Island was Mrs Hazel Luce from Portland in Oregon, U.S.A., who spent a few hours ashore while the passenger ship, *Waiben*, was in port at T.I. She distinguished herself by catching a forty-two pound cod while fishing near Hocking's jetty. She landed the giant herself, a catch that would have delighted any experienced fisherman.

Attached to the Hocking's town home is an historical museum housing relics of the Torres Straits that date back over a hundred years. Mrs Hocking showed me an invitation card dated 1898, yellow with age, addressed to Mr Hocking's late uncle which read, "Mr and Mrs James Clark invite you to afternoon tea on board the *Wanetta*." At that time the English migrant ship, the *Wanetta*, was anchored in Brisbane while on her maiden voyage and Mr Hocking decided to take the ship's name for the newly-formed Torres Strait Pearling Company.

A leisurely walk from the Hocking's holiday home to the hilltop lighthouse station is a memorable adventure. When I took the inland track for the first time, I was forewarned by Mrs Hocking to "stop and look behind at the highest hill before descending." Even so, I was unprepared for the breath-taking view. Immediately, I remembered Robert Louis Stevenson's words, "Have you in all your travels far, seen a land more passing fair?"

In the glacier-like surface of the blue water below, the little island of Wai-Wer, rose up amid the sea's immensity half way between Goode Island and Thursday Island. It was surrounded by distant green islands and along its shores were palm trees growing above a white ribbon stretch of beach. From the summit of the highest hill on Wai-Wer, a doll-like white house peeped up into the sky. I knew then what an English naval officer had meant when he had gazed out on the snowfields of north-eastern Victoria and said, "If I could play the piano, I would paint that scene." I felt that way about this seascape.

The island of Wai-Wer was sometimes called "Look-Out" and the little island was used for this purpose in the early days. Tribal man climbed to the highest point to direct fellow men to the feeding grounds of the dugong.

Before the first World War, Wai-Wer island was known appropriately as Honeymoon Island. Newly-married couples rented the house from a T.I. resident who held the lease of the island and honeymooners took over an island in the Pacific. But times change and young people getting married prefer now to go south. The old house has long ago fallen into bad repair.

Goode Island seemed suitably named and I wondered if Matthew Flinders had combined sentiment with the conviction that he found the island "good" when he named it.

Unfortunately the original name has been tampered with over the years and during the second World War the final letter was dropped from the name and the letter "s" substituted. At present, the island still retains the war name of Goods Island but many people prefer the name bestowed on it by Flinders.

In his discovery of Goode Island, Matthew Flinders looked into the future not into the past like his illustrious grandson, the late Sir William Matthew Flinders Petrie. I met this famous archaeologist while I was serving with the 2nd A.I.F. Nursing Service in the Middle East during the second World War. At eighty-six years of age he was living in retirement at the American School of Oriental Research headquarters in Jerusalem. A distinguished figure resembling a biblical patriarch, with thick snowy white hair and flowing white beard, he welcomed visits from Australian Service personnel to whom the name of Matthew Flinders had been well known since school days.

Sir Flinders Petrie had made a name for himself in England as a pioneer of biblical archaeology. He spent fifty

115

years excavating in Palestine and Egypt with remarkable results. I spent an unforgettable hour in the company of this man, absorbing mind pictures of excavated long-buried cities and ancient palaces dating back to the time of the pharaohs. I received a treasure myself, an autographed copy of a stimulating little book, *Vision of the Ages*.

In speaking of Australia, Sir Flinders Petrie was quick to recall the controversy over a memorial to his navigator grandfather. In 1922 he had offered to present intimate letters and documents of his grandfather to the first Australian state to honour his grandfather's name in a fitting memorial. The offer set off a controversy as to which state had the first right. Finally, it was decided that New South Wales should erect the memorial and valuable letters and documents are now preserved for future generations in the Mitchell Library, Sydney.

19

FOR SHELL LOVERS

THE WEALTH OF THURSDAY ISLAND lies in the rich surrounding waters and the largest pearl shell beds in the world are to be found between Cape York and New Guinea.

Take one large, hard, concave oyster shell and you will find it lined with a silver sheen of exquisite iridescent mother of pearl, finished with silver, gold, or black edging, and if you are lucky you might find a pearl.

The pearling industry was once a great industry but over the years its activities have been curtailed by the development of cheaper plastics and synthetics. Specimens of the king of shells continue to gleam from home shelves in different countries of the world and the Torres Strait pearl shell still finds a market in the U.S.A. and other countries where there is manufacturing of superior quality buttons, studs, and trinkets.

The Torres Strait pearling industry also handles the humble trochus shell for export. The cone-shaped white shell with heavy overlay of pink stripes is found in abundance on coral reefs and in shallow waters of the Strait but they must not be taken until a certain size.

Many of the T.I. residents and visitors have made a hobby of collecting and it is not unusual to see shell museums or specimens displayed on lounge room shelves. Photographers consider the tropical shells excellent material for slides and some have specialised in shell arrangements or shell photographs.

Mr Reg Scott, an amateur conchologist, has lived on T.I. for many years and is the undisputed Shell King of the Torres Strait. His collection is valued at thousands of dollars. To an enthusiast such as Reg Scott, shell collecting is a way of life and as a teetotaller he maintains that he "would rather collect shells than bottle tops."

He exchanges shells with overseas collectors, and on one occasion he returned from a short visit down south to find 140 items of correspondence awaiting his attention. His shortest communication was from an old lady who had written on half a sheet of paper and enclosed a one pound note to cover the cost of the required specimen. She addressed the envelope simply: "Shell Collector, Thursday Island, Australia."

The longest communication ran to several pages of typewritten foolscap paper. Many collectors write to Reg Scott of their own initiative by taking his name from the shell publications. Others have their names taken by Reg Scott from the Directory of Conchologists, a Who's Who of shell collectors, published in U.S.A., and circulated throughout 120 countries. It contains the names of hundreds of shell collectors.

A quiet, serious-minded man with a dry sense of humour, Reg Scott started collecting shells years ago. He is an active member of the Malacology (Molluscs) Society of Australia and writes to thirty overseas conchologists. He keeps up correspondence with many pen-friends whose hobby is shell collecting. Retired bank managers, wealthy Americans, teenagers, and enthusiasts from all walks of life, the rich, the poor, the young, the old, write to Reg Scott. One conchologist writer is part-owner of one of America's largest shell factories and that business represents over five million dollars yearly.

Reg Scott lived with his second wife, Thelma, and small daughter, Winifred, in a house appropriately called the Shell Sanctuary. For five days of the week he worked as an engineer at the local government electric power house and collected shells at the weekends and on holidays. A likeable, middle-aged man of medium height, very muscular and incredibly suntanned, Reg Scott is a cockney by birth, born within the sound of Bow Bells. He grew up to become an engine driver. At the age of seven he came to Australia with his parents and first lived at Mackay in Queensland. Reg Scott loved the sea and became proficient in handling fishing gear and even learned to perform a high trapeze act over water.

At the age of thirteen he found that his first underwater activity paid off well. The men playing in a local "Two Up School" suddenly "got wind" that the police were on their trail; they threw the coins into the river and rushed off along its banks. Reg threw off his shirt, jumped into the water, and retrieved much of the money. From this novel introduction to underwater activity, he became an expert skin diver and fisherman and even fashioned his own underwater gear in the days when spearfishing was a little known art in Australia. In a series of adventures with Mother Nature over the years, Reg Scott has suffered bad body burns, broken bones, and shipwreck. These experiences have tended to make a man of his calibre start all over again. Once, he and his former wife and stepson were marooned for over eighteen weeks on a deserted part of the north Queensland coast. In a Robinson Crusoe existence the trio lived well on food dug from the ground and were kept alive by yams, arrowroot, crabs, fish, and birds.

Reg Scott has many good stories to tell, including a number about his time aboard the luxurious motor launch, the *Royal Flight*. He was chosen in the early 1940s to be engineer aboard the boat that had been hired by the Arthur Rank film company to transport officials, actors, and crew to Fiji for the making of *Blue Lagoon*.

I would like to digress for a moment to recall an encounter with one of the actors of this particular film, five years ago from when I am writing this. On my journey across the channel to Ireland from Liverpool in England my fellow passenger was Noel Purcell, the crusty old sailor and protector of the two ship-wrecked children in the film *Blue Lagoon*. He was celebrating at that time the Grand National horse race which had been run that day for the last time on the famous race course near Liverpool. He was, I remember with amusement, a different man from the film character he so well portrayed.

When Reg Scott was in Fiji he had built to his own specifications the twenty-five feet long, fast motor launch, the *Minni Ha-Ha*, which was later sold for use at a tourist resort in north Queensland. His most treasured reminders of the happy time spent in Fiji include an autographed photo of Jean Simmons and references from the director of Pagewood Studios.

As all shells are nocturnal in their habits, moving around freely and feeding at night, Reg Scott sometimes rises at 3 a.m. to search for shell specimens. He takes his dog, Chillie, with him. Since a boy of eleven, Reg Scott has taken a dog with him in lonely, hazardous places. For shell collecting he says that a good night light is an essential part of his equipment, for direction is sometimes difficult to determine out on the reefs. His most prized acquisition was a brass, cone-shaped container, like a cocktail shaker, that had been fixed to the top of a four foot long pole. This was called a tonga torch and he had had it sent from America. It was a practical, inexpensive light that burned for nine hours on one pint of kerosene. Before beginning his searches on lonely reefs at night, he sank the pole into the sand so that the elevated light served as a reference point during his meanderings to lonely places after specimens.

Indoors, Reg Scott was often to be found with his head down over one of his thumbed through volumes on shells. If shell collectors just beginning wish to emulate Reg then might I suggest that they look at some of the books he had used frequently for reference and pleasure: *Dictionary of Shells, American Sea Shells, The Shell Book, Review of the Voludae, Shell Life, Shellfish of New Zealand, World*

120

Cowries, and there were two handbooks for collectors. Most were illustrated with beautiful photographs of shells. His most treasured book, a gift from a South African friend, is a serious thesis on the scallop shell. It is a beautifully bound red leather volume that measures fifteen inches by nine inches. The cover is embossed with multiple gold insignia of the familiar ribbed Pecten or scallop shell and I thought it fitting artistry to commemorate the Golden Jubilee of the International Shell Transport and Trading Company for which it was published.

The scallop shell was first adopted as a symbol and later as a registered trade mark by the founder of the company, Marcus Samuel, who with his brother accepted it as the company badge and name. Later, trading ships took on the names of various specimens of shells.

This sculptured shell, perfectly hinged to open like a jewel box, has influenced mankind throughout the ages. It is to be found in Greek mythology and at a later period of history was used in a coat-of-arms for nobility. It has even been traced to South America where, in one thousand B.C., the early inhabitants of the area where Chile now stands adopted the scallop shell as their motif.

20

AN UNFORGETTABLE EVENING

YEARS AGO, IN INLAND AUSTRALIA where the skyline is unbroken and stars seem more brilliant than elsewhere, I learned of galaxy formations. My teacher then was a cattle station manager who proved to be a keen observer and reader of astronomy. I was reminded of him when I met Reg Scott.

Each fortnight Reg placed an advertisement in the local newspaper inviting residents, visitors, and tourists to inspect his collection. I went along with an English doctor from the T.I. hospital, a Swedish couple, Annette and Raglund, and the senior radio operator of coastal communications, Gray McDonald. Reg and Thelma Scott met us at the door of their home and we followed them into the collection room. We sat around a table and for three hours watched in awe as drawer after drawer of shells was taken from a near-by cabinet and displayed on the table in front of us. In all we saw forty drawers. Each drawer contained several rows of a particular shell and its beauty was shown off by a smooth black velvet backing. We were moved to sudden cries of admiration and eager questions. We wanted to know the origin, the value of the shells, and how they were produced.

We learned that there were 50,000 kinds of known shells in fresh, brackish, tropical and Arctic waters, and that shells were given latin names as this language was still in use when the shells were named. Reg Scott admitted he did not know the names of all shells he handled but then, "Who does?" he added. He wanted to catalogue his collection at some later date. Shells come from eggs or spawn laid in capsules. These tiny inhabitants, as they grow, build around them their houses with their different patterns, curves, spines, and colours. Shells are mainly of two kinds: the univalves and the bivalves. Nearly all univalves have apertures on the right side but there is one known exception to the rule of righthandedness. This is the *Fulger perverse* which shell books show as having the aperture on the left side. Of the two categories of shells the bivalves were thought to be the more numerous.

I was entranced with the colours of the shells: the deep purples, the vivid reds, oranges, tangerines, cyclamen shades, pinks. My first comment was that the shells had been painted but Reg Scott countered this with, "And who do you think the marine artist would be?" I was rather subdued after that.

Thelma Scott used the shells to make jewellery, vases, and even handbags. A beautiful white handbag, round in shape, and made entirely from shells, weighed two and a half pounds. Most of her things she sold to tourists but there was a hairband of *Cytaca monita* shells that had been given to her. The shells, commonly called "money cowries" and used as a substitute for money in primitive areas of New Guinea, came from a Norwegian seaman who had been helped by her husband.

Annette, the Swedish visitor in our group, was interested in relating colour and design to materials. She hoped to see the original patterns and the brilliant and muted colours of the shells transferred to silks and satins.

Most shells, when found, have a thin outer covering called "periostracum" which can be removed with acid and water. The shell is then washed in clean water, dried, and rubbed with a vegetable oil which soaks into the surface, highlighting markings and natural colours and helping to preserve brittle shell. Cowries, olive, and pencil shells are three families free for the most part of nature's camouflage.

If shell specimens are to be prepared properly, considerable time and a certain amount of skill and knowledge are required of the collector. Shells should be alive, undamaged, and without blemishes before a collector begins to work with them.

How a tiny creature inside a shell made such classical spines, orderly curves, and different colours was always puzzling to me and I was somewhat tremulous in handling the Pearly Nautilus. This seemed to me to rival any of Man's intricate designs or examples of his engineering ability. The Pearly Nautilus is a bivalve consisting of two halves, each perfect in details to resemble miniature turbine wheels. The chambers were joined together by a tube and the inhabitant of the shell, a member of the octopus family, lived permanently in the last chamber. The tube provided the means for the tiny animal to fill and empty each chamber with sea water so that the shell could sink or float. The outer covering of the shell is mother-of-pearl and it is from this that the shell gets its name. In numbers the Pearly Nautilus has commercial value. It is not a protected shell and in the Torres Strait and other parts of the world perfect specimens are eagerly sought after by shell collectors.

In the same family and also highly prized is the white Paper Nautilus. It is not really a shell but a delicate egg sac made by a mollusc that resembles the common squid with its many arms. It is like an open cradle with lacy interior and serrated edges. The mollusc clasps this to her body to lay eggs in and when they are hatched, the fragile sac is discarded and floats away. How this delicate object survives the tumult of the ocean is a great marine mystery.

One shell that builds its own buoyant raft to keep it afloat is the tiny Violet or Foam shell. Its float is formed from air-filled vesicles attached to the foot of the mollusc.

Some of the strangest and most valuable shells are dredged from the sea at depths of 2,000 feet. The *Ranella pulchra* shell for example, which on one side is the shape of a kookaburra and on the other the shape of a maple leaf. It is dredged from waters near Gladstone in Queensland and belongs to the Harp family of shells found usually in the prawning grounds of the southern Queensland coast. The *Ranella pulchra* is easily identified by its fifteen ridges and its mottled colours of brown, pink, and black.

The Great Barrier Reef, stretching for 1,300 miles along the coast of north Queensland, is recognised as the best shell ground in the world. Not only is it prolific in shells but it contains some of the world's most colourful examples. For collectors, part of the beauty of shells lies in the fusion of colour, the design of concentric and parallel lines, sculptured furbelows, flounces, protrusions, and spot markings.

One of the most popular shells is the cowrie of which there are more than 300 species. When first taken from the water the cowrie has a glossy surface. It is a shell that delights children. Held to the ear it gives out the sound of the ocean and its rounded back and under-teeth seem made for exploratory fingers and small pockets. Some have muted spots which resemble the markings and colours of a tortoise-shell cat, and others are in the soft shades of a spotted fawn or persian cat. The allover rich brown cowrie is highly regarded by collectors and the Tiger Cowrie is common to many homes.

Some species of cowrie are rare; the Golden Cowrie was said to bring 200 U.S.A. dollars several years ago. Cowries are to be found almost right along the east coast of Australia, and although in the past fifteen years many of their breeding grounds and young have been destroyed by careless collectors leaving rocks upturned, there have been some remarkable finds by men working dredges. A perfect white cowrie, five inches long, was dredged from a depth of nearly 2,000 feet in Bass Strait.

In parts of New Guinea shells are used in bartering and for decoration. Women attach small cowries to bilums (hold-alls made of native fibre) and these hang down a wearer's back from a forehead band. As the dancers sway and move the shells come together, bell-like.

The Bu Shell, found in the Torres Strait, and used on some islands to call worshippers to prayer, is the largest marine bivalve known to conchologists. A great booming sound comes from the shell once a small hole has been pierced in the shell's apex and this is blown into.

The Baler shell of the Torres Strait and Barrier Reef area grows to a huge size too. It is used by Islanders to bale water from canoes, and tourists find it a useful lamp base or flower container. On the outside it is a dark brown shell with black markings but the interior is a rich apricot colour.

For me the most beautiful shells in Reg Scott's collection were the Angel's Wings, or more strictly *Pholas costata.* Each was an unblemished white, delicately-ribbed shell with an all-over raised pattern resembling old fashioned crochet work. Reg proudly showed us each perfect half, seven inches in length, shaped like the outspread wing of an angel. It was difficult to realise that these exquisite pieces came from mud flats and had lain buried in several inches of mud.

The waters of the Great Barrier Reef, Booby Island in the Torres Strait, and the Fijian Islands are excellent collecting grounds for the Turbo shells. Reg Scott, like most of us in the north, had gathered together as many of the stoppers to these shells as he could find. To children and adults alike they were cat's eyes. These stone-like shells with their green, black, and white markings, were often polished and mounted on rings, brooches, and bracelets.

Shell jewellery was extremely popular but even the body scales of the garfish were put to artistic use. Reg showed us a string of pale pink artificial pearls made from scales which had been dipped into a pearly paste. The tiniest item in his collection was a minute, lustrous seed pearl that would have to be X-rayed before its value was known.

The young Swedish freelance writer, Raglund, had a particular flair for underwater photography and the natural colours of the shell collection fired him into immediately planning his next excursion. For the English doctor there was a sudden burst of interest in the workings of the shells. The *Cardium cordessa*, a univalve commonly known as the "heart cockle," was of convex shape on one side but concave on the other. With an opening down the middle the shell structure was somewhat puzzling in that there seemed no exit for the small animal. Each of us had our questions and the radio operator, Gray McDonald, demonstrated that his interest lay mainly in the engineering feats of the intricate Pearly Nautilus and in the natural hinges of the bivalve, *Spondylus gusonia*, a Mexican shell commonly called the Mermaid's Jewel Box. This was an ornate sculptured shell which opened on a natural hinge to reveal a shiny white interior edged with red and brown.

We were all familiar with the common Conus shell. With the periostrum removed it is a patterned, colourful shell. It looks quite harmless but the thick shell-covering houses a poisonous barb. Usually this remains inactive even when the shell is lightly disturbed, but the barb acts as a defence mechanism to combat stronger or more direct irritants. Islanders and collectors learn how to handle the shell but deaths have been recorded.

The following account was printed in the Townsville newspaper of the time and records one incident in north Queensland:

When the fishing party of eleven well-known Ayr residents received a happy send-off at the railway station on their departure for a cruise of the Whitsunday Passage no one dreamt that the expedition would end so tragically.

The full story of the circumstances surrounding the tragedy was revealed to our representative who interviewed Mr J. Breen shortly after his return to Ayr on Thursday.

The party had spent six days cruising islands of the Great Barrier Reef in the launch owned by Mr Bruce Jamieson, of Bowen, and had gone out to Bushy Island. They were making a leisurely return and on reaching Hayman Island where there is a nice reef from which water ebbs, leaving myriads of shells of all sizes and descriptions, the party decided to make a stop and collect specimens. Every man in the party left the launch to gather shells and all returned to the launch for lunch. Charles Garbold finished lunch first and immediately went up on deck to examine his shells, picking up a conus shell about three and a half inches long and one and a half inches in circumference. In order to discover its pattern and colouring he turned it over on his left hand and began scraping the surface of its camouflaging covering when he felt a sting in the centre of his palm. Mr Breen joined him on deck about five minutes later and showing him the shell Charlie said, "This shell stung me," and went on to tell what happened. A second later he said, "Do you know my hand is so numb you could cut it off with a knife and I wouldn't feel it." The two men sat side by side while Charlie pointed out the prong of the shell from which the sting had issued. Presently, he began to feel all over his lips and mouth and complained of numbness, informing his companion, "I can't see the hut on the island." He was at once taken below to the cabin and given a dose of brandy and he said he could not see out of the window. Offered another dose of brandy he shook his head, managing to mumble something including the word "choke" and never spoke again.

Alarmed at the turn of events the anxious party made a twenty mile dash to Cannon Valley. Fortunately a truck was drawn up on the beach to which the sufferer was transferred with Messrs Breen and Gray in attendance. Meanwhile another member of the party lost no time in telephoning the doctor at Proserpine, fifteen miles away, who came out immediately in the ambulance. Charlie was alive but obviously in a critical condition being almost paralysed. On reaching Proserpine it was found he had passed away. It was stated that poison from the barbed sting of the shell had affected his nerves and flown to the brain, the victim being unable to speak or move within an hour after the happening although he appeared to suffer no pain.

21

POSSESSION ISLAND

TO THINK OF POSSESSION ISLAND is to think of Captain James Cook. The north-west side of this lushly vegetated island faces Endeavour Strait and it is through that strait, the only entrance through the Great Barrier Reef to the coast of Australia, that Captain Cook sailed. With some of his men he landed on the island in 1770, climbed the 400 feet to the summit, raised the British flag, claimed the Torres Strait for the Crown, and ordered a salute of guns from his ship H.M.S. *Endeavour*.

The cairn of stone remained on the summit until some years ago and was used as a vantage point for viewing the tip of Cape York Peninsula which was three miles away. It is believed by some that Cook buried records on Possession Island; others claim that the area has been dug over and no trace of them found.

At one time a gold reef was traced up to the summit where Cook raised the flag and a flourishing gold mine was operated on the island. No gold has been found there for thirty years but it is interesting to speculate what would have happened if Captain Cook had discovered gold on

Possession Island. Australia might then have developed from the north and not from the south.

Around Possession Island the seas are so rough that at high tide it is impossible for fishermen or travellers to land.

Oysters nearly six inches across cover rocks along the shoreline and at low tide the rocky outcrops and headlands are favoured fishing spots. There are many tales of fish that snapped the lines but one T.I. fisherman took home a forty-two-pound mackerel he had landed on the rocks of the island.

Coconut palms imported from Java grow just above the shoreline, native orchids wrap themselves around trees and nestle into trunks, and Possession Island, with its profusion of exotic flowering trees, plants and shrubs, is a botanist's paradise.

In 1926 the Royal Historical Society erected a memorial commemorating Captain Cook's landing on Possession Island. The story of this event was told to me by Charles Garvey, one of the three men engaged in the project.

The summit where Cook raised the flag was the obvious place for the memorial but as Charles Garvey put it "there was no water up there to mix the cement and it was a five ton monument." The Royal Geographical Society supplied the mould, inscription plate, and several valuable sheets of blueprint and the men carried sand—and more sand—from the beach to the solid granite rock sixty feet up from where Cook landed. Sixteen bags of cement were used and water was brought to the surface by block and tackle from an old near-by mining shaft.

When completed according to plan the monument stood six feet high on a base four feet by four, set into pointed, jagged rocks, facing out to sea. The inscription plate was set in the mortar and an empty whisky bottle containing the bluesheets and the names of the three construction men went into the middle.

Charles Garvey commented that the papers could be valuable in a thousand years and no cyclone on earth would shift that monument. The monument stands as a lasting tribute to the courage and skill of those sailors who, two hundred years ago, guided a small vessel through the unknown and treacherous waters of the Strait.

The inscription plate reads:

Lieutenant James Cook Of The 'Endeavour'
Landed On This Island Which He Called Possession Island
And In The Name Of King George III
Took Possession Of The East Coast Of Australia
From Latitude 58 South Of This Place
August 22nd, 1770.

Charles Garvey recalled incidents as though they had happened that minute and not thirty years ago. "The sea was pretty rough round Possession the day we arrived to start the job," he said. "But somehow we managed to land on the beach and on the first night my mates decided to sleep ashore in the open. They put down a tarpaulin beneath a large almond tree. Funny thing, though, those blokes didn't seem to mind the idea of snakes crawling around."

He was a laconic chap but even so I was prompted to ask if there were really snakes on the island.

"Sure," he replied calmly. "You'll always find snakes where there is gold."

He left the boys on the shore and went aboard the launch to sleep. He tossed all night with his boat on the rough sea but felt himself better off than the blokes ashore. At midnight the rain pelted down and there is no doubt that he watched as gleefully as if they had been in a corroboree for him. His supply of anecdotes seemed endless and there was little reason to doubt that he might have initiated some of the adventures. There was, for example, his story of the survey ship, H.M.S. *Fantom*.

It anchored offshore from Possession Island while Charles Garvey and his men were working there. All was peaceful even after twenty naval chaps landed and set up camp but then one day, pandemonium. A sudden fire in the bush swept hordes of black and brown snakes into the new camp. Up jumped the chart-making crew, with sudden scamperings, shrieks of terror, and violent accusations.

"The British Skipper, Commander Maxwell, was an

131

awfully nice chap. He enjoyed going all tropical when off duty and relaxing in a lava lava," added Garvey.

The Commander also kept a tame black pig called Dennis aboard ship and when the *Fantom* left, Dennis was left to Charles Garvey. Charles Garvey explained the event this way, "Well, fat pigs aren't quite in my line as pets. What would you expect us to do but make quick work of that porker and bury his bones in the sand!"

I pictured the *Fantom* sailing quietly into the distance.

My first view of Possession Island was from the Harbour Master's launch as it cruised in close to Cape York. The hills of the island loomed over the tip of the cape almost as though they were part of the mainland.

Cape York looked all virgin bush but fifteen miles down from the tip a model native town had been set up on a government reserve.

Bamaga's history dates back to 1947 and a movement of Torres Strait Islanders from swamp land on Saibu Island near the New Guinea coast. When the low-lying areas on Saibu became infested with malarial mosquitoes the Islanders moved south to a place called Muttee Head on Cape York Peninsula. In 1951 the Queensland Government moved them to a better site eleven miles north. A site for a permanent native settlement was selected and the area blessed by a native Torres Strait Anglican priest, Father Francis Bowie. Like Moses of old, the chief tribesman, Bamaga, led his four hundred people to the new site. He did not live to see the setting-up of the new town with its European-type houses, the timber mills, and school.

No white person is allowed on the native settlement without permission from the Department of Native Affairs but in 1960 visitors flocked in from surrounding areas, with government approval, to see the town's third Annual Rodeo and Agricultural Show.

On the first day of the show hurricane-like winds prevented boats from setting out from T.I. but on the second day the water was scarcely stirred by the gentle breeze. Ten boats, crowded with Islanders, tourists and administration staff from the hospital and offices, left the

T.I. wharf at 7 a.m. for Cape York. Women dressed casually but observed the ruling that shorts were best not worn on native reserves. Slacks, jeans, skirts, and blouses, or simple cotton frocks were the order of the day. Settlement administration was quite explicit in this request and on Palm Island mini shifts two inches above the knee were thought unsuitable by the local school headmaster. Gathered skirts of mid-calf length were advocated and newcomers to the Island were asked to wear knee-length robes over bathing costumes. Newcomers to the Torres Straits on this excursion to Bamaga dressed comfortably and were prepared for the clouds of fine red dust on the mainland dirt roads.

The Government launch took the hospital superintendent, his wife and three daughters, the nursing sisters and hospital employees to Bamaga but other privately-owned boats were hired out for the day. One, carrying fifteen passengers, charged a hundred dollars.

The journey from T.I. took three and a half hours and for part of it I chatted to Nicholas, the bare-footed Islander coxswain. He had been born at Cape York and knew Jack McLaren, the Australian author of adventure books. He was, he said, related by blood. The story of Jack McLaren's years as the only white man on Cape York Peninsula is told in his book *My Crowded Solitude*. In 1911 he cleared three hundred acres of scrub country, established a coconut plantation, developed a copra industry, and employed men who had never seen a white man before.

The boats pulled in at an old stone jetty at Red Island Point, nearest port to the old wartime airfield, named Jacky Jacky after the faithful Aboriginal boy of the Edward Kennedy expedition. Jacky Jacky airfield was built by American Negroes during the second World War. Nearly two miles long and with more than forty dispersal bays it was an important airbase in the defence of Australia. Nowadays, the airstrip is only used occasionally.

A government truck met the boats and ran a four-mile shuttle service for the Show visitors who scrambled into the back of the vehicle and were covered in red dust on reaching the showgrounds.

22

BAMAGA

THE STRETCH OF COUNTRY from Red Island Point on the coast to Bamaga four miles inland provided plenty of contrast for the visitor. Vegetation was thick and lush but broken occasionally by six feet high red sandhills. Overhead big-winged brown birds wheeled uneasily away towards further distant trees at the sound of the truck or person. The thirty feet wide red dirt road pushed its way sharply through the bush and only here and there were there glimpses of the Overland Telegraph Line. A black and white sign proclaimed "Nona Creek" and a short distance after that lay the settlement of Bamaga and through this the road sprawled on another half mile to the Showgrounds entrance. It halted at the sign: Welcome To Bamaga. Industrial and Agricultural Sub-Department. D.N.A. The framed timber archway supporting the sign opened into the Bamaga recreation grounds. Usually the venue for horse racing, cycling, and sporting fixtures it had at show time been taken over by vegetable, handicraft, and display stalls.

Settlement residents and visitors jostled to get a better

look at what the local community farms had produced and the vegetables were stacked up high on shelves protected side and top by coconut palm fronds. In another stall boomerangs, spears, woven floor mats, baskets and fans made from fine grasses were on show.

Visitors from T.I. and the Australian cities inevitably chose to buy from the "Modern Handicrafts" stall. What caught their eye before the embroidered pillowcases and handkerchiefs were the brightly coloured, lace-edged men's briefs. They were elaborately decorated with simple-stitched designs and were meant to be worn under grass skirts in ceremonial dances.

School children, never far from their models of boats, maps, woven handkerchiefs, paintings and carved weapons, idly amused themselves by counting the visitors or looking for quieter places to run and chase. Small possums came out from under shirts and round eyes and lips of bare-footed boys called to the twelve fat, black pigs on display.

Children rarely went into the crowded shed-cum-restaurant but some waited around ready to run messages for the Bamaga women who worked steadily serving two course meals or light refreshments.

At the rear of the restaurant a boxing ring attracted crowds of men, women, and children. A mid-day match with a prize of a silver cup and four dollars had been arranged and the contestants went into the ring right on time. Tony Doolan, a small mainland Aboriginal, with negroid features and straight unkempt hair, wore only an old pair of khaki shorts and brown leather belt but his opponent, Arthur Ketchell, a Torres Strait Islander, came out fresh, spirited, and wearing black boxing boots and black satin shorts. A T.I. policeman moved into the ring with a stop watch in his hand and the fight was on.

"Give it to 'im Tony! Give it to 'im hard!" the crowd roared as the Aboriginal moved swiftly about the ring in bare feet, niftily avoiding blows. A knockout came a few rounds later when the fiery mainlander sent the Islander thudding to the floor with one heavy blow. The crowd yelled with excitement as Tony Doolan's hand was raised.

There was an almost immediate dispersal of people as Torres Strait onlookers ambled off to find the shade. Midday heat was greater on the mainland than in the Straits and with red dust seeping through hair and clothes Islanders began to feel a little disgruntled.

In the early afternoon Aboriginal stockmen, flamboyant in red cotton shirts, long trousers, cowboy hats, and elasticised boots sat astride bullocks. Man and beast rarely got to the end of the field but cheering for one man overlapped with cheering for the next.

The highlight of the Show, the Bamaga Cup, was run over two laps with seven horses. When the horses were lined up, the crowd quiet, a helicopter whirred overhead and swooped down to land. Islanders and Aborigines scattered and the pilot and his two passengers from Weipa waved happily until a cloud of red dust blocked the landing spot. The helicopter rose higher, circled the area, whirled away to land elsewhere while the horses ran and the spectators lined the railings again.

The winning jockey had been released from jail to ride that day and he rushed across the line on a great prancing brown horse called Comet. The Director of Native Affairs, Mr Pat Killoran, handed the cup, a gift of the Minister of Health for Queensland, Dr Noble, to the wife of the superintendent at Bamaga. She presented it to the winner and he returned to jail.

Bamaga Settlement consisted of neat rows of houses on stilts. These were surrounded by well-kept gardens and vegetable plots. Houses inside were clean and tidy and it was a task of the resident native policeman to inspect for cleanliness and order. If the residents of the rent-free houses were found to be careless they were called before the local council.

Men were employed on community farms and in building and plumbing. On the farms there were government-organised experiments with maize and other types of grain, the growing of different grasses for soil improvement, and an irrigation project was being developed. About twenty thousand gallons of water were brought by engine and pump from the cement dams at Nona Creek which supplied the town with domestic water as well.

Children and adults were forbidden to bathe in the lower reaches of the town's only creek and for Island people whose previous way of life had centred around the sea, self-discipline had to be strong. Their natural playgrounds for swimming, fishing, and duck shooting were the waters around Red Island Point jetty and the Jardine River which was near by.

Seventy-six coloured children and one white child attended the Bamaga school. The primary school was staffed in 1960 by Islanders and instruction in handicrafts was of a very high standard. The school later came under the Queensland Education Department.

Women at that time either went to the T.I. hospital to have their babies or stayed at home in the care of a native midwife. A hospital of ten beds was planned for Bamaga and at Show time it had been built, with local timber and cement floors, but was not ready for occupation. It was to be staffed by a European trained nurse and native assistants.

Government employees of the Department of Native Affairs lived in substantially built houses beyond the bridge spanning Nona Creek. They were dependent on each other for company and the annual Show was the event of the year bringing in news of the outside world.

The superintendent of the settlement, Mr Hamilton, was a keen horticulturalist and tended fields of citrus trees. He screened films twice a week for residents of the settlement who sat on forms to watch westerns, cartoons, and documentaries. The westerns met with loud shouts of approval and at Show time in 1960 a meteorology officer from T.I., Mr John Hyndman, introduced a new form of entertainment with puppetry. The Big Bad Wolf, Snow White, and other traditional characters bounced out at the audience who were at first puzzled by the actions and language but then took happily to the activity.

Bamaga's only sawmill meets the building needs of the Gulf Country and the Torres Straits. Timber is milled mainly from the bloodwoods, messmates, sollygums, and the Leichhardt Pine. This pine is the only tree of the area resistant to white ants. By 1960, thirty-six thousand super feet of timber had been milled and taken out of the area.

The manager of the mill was of Scottish ancestry and had kept his broad accent after thirty years in Australia. He lived alone with his ten year old son and employed a coloured girl to do the work. At Show time he kept open house for visitors.

He was the only white man at the mill and found the casualness of workers frustrating at times. According to Scotty, even the regular workers were unpredictable. They downed tools at any hour of the day and he was left with a contract and no labour. Workers were paid the basic wage and their families were well fed.

He sent his son to the local school and encouraged him to spend holidays and weekends exploring the bush with the settlement children.

Graham, the son, was obviously a boy of considerable sporting prowess. Around the walls of the cottage were cups for swimming and diving that had been won at north Queensland schools at an earlier time. Even so, the bush children promised each time to look after the boy and the father knew they could.

Like many people of the far north who were close to the sea Scotty collected shells. When tides and weather were suitable he searched the coastline along Cape York. The verandah of his house might be compared with the rocky headland on an undulating coast but instead of providing a vantage point for tourists to survey the bays and hills and reefs it was a means of taking in with a sweeping glance the activities of the settlement.

In front, row upon row of citrus trees were growing steadily, flowering, bearing the beginnings of fruit and in season cabbages, tomatoes, cucumbers and melons formed a patchwork quilt. To the left stood the town store which stocked groceries, clothing, and tobacco.

Small box-like buildings in the distance made up the piggery. It was rumoured that Bamaga pork offered for sale through the Island Industries Board of the Department of Native Affairs fetched several dollars a pound in T.I. Beyond the piggery of Bamaga lay the bush of Cape York and some of the most rugged country in Australia. Men from the settlement went inland occasionally to round up some of the wild pigs and cattle but for the most part the beasts were allowed to multiply and range the rough areas in peace.

Strewn with reefs, the waters of the north are dangerous at night even to those who know the areas well. Visitors to Bamaga left Red Island Point in the late afternoon. They were watched by an elderly coloured man who was neatly dressed in khaki trousers and shirt. Through whisperings I learned that he was Enoch, a Saibu Islander, a man who had given the Government a lot of trouble. He was said to be an expert at puri puri and a look in the eye from him could shrivel a person up. Bamaga residents thought of him with varying amounts of fear.

As the boat pulled out from the jetty the Torres Strait Island word for greeting—Yo-wah! Yo-wah!—echoed across the waters and close in to the mainland, on top of a pearling lugger, a native boy dived for the departing visitors.

It was the end of a memorable day, a stimulating experience enjoyed in an exotic atmosphere and in an environment of successful enterprise. The difficulty of populating a far northern area, practically uninhabited twenty years before, had been surmounted. Bamaga was almost a miracle. It was a heartwarming experiment that resulted in a successful adjustment of a simple island people to civilized way of life. Future generations will come to regard Bamaga as their ancestral home. Legends and pageantry will grow up around the name of the faithful Mamoose who voluntarily and under protection of the Government, led his people from their island home to start a permanent settlement on the mainland of Cape York Peninsula.